THE DIVINE SIGNIFICANCE OF BEING AN INTROVERT

PAROMITA GANGULI

Made with ♥ on the Notion Press Platform
www.notionpress.com

"Whoever is delighted in solitude is either a wild beast or a
God"

- Aristotle

Contents

Preface ix

Prologue xiii

Acknowledgements xvii

Part 1

1. Myths Vs Reality 3

***

2. The Dunning-Kruger Effect: An Interesting Glimpse 9
   Into The Human Mind

***

3. Sacred Solitude: The Spiritual Concept Of Isolation 15

***

4. Protection From Low Vibrational Energies 23

***

5. Creation Of A Beast-Mindset 29

***

6. The Phoenix Method 35

***

7. Success For Introverts 43

***

8. Soul Connections: The Only Relationships We Need 51

***

9. Awareness: The Bulletproof Mindset 57

***

10. The Impact Consciousness 63

Contents

***

11. Emotional Intelligence   69

***

12. Sensitivity: The Gift Of Empathy   75

***

13. The Subliminal Healer And Peace Maker   81

***

14. Self Talk: Conversations With The Divine   87

***

15. The Age Of Aquarius   93

***

Part 2

16. Sound Healing: High Frequency Music   101

17. Use The Power Of Words   107

18. Practice Slow Mornings   114

19. Morning Nature Walks   118

20. Solo Retreats   120

21. Meditation + Art   125

22. Journaling: Record Your Meaningful Insights   129

23. Declutter Your Space   135

24. Routine And Flexibility   142

25. Exercise For Introverts   147

Part 3

26. The Quiet Genius—Albert Einstein's Introverted   155

Contents

Brilliance

27. Marie Curie - The Quiet Innovator   159

28. J.K. Rowling-The Quiet Magician Of Imagination   163

29. Bill Gates - The Quiet Visionary Behind The Screen   167

30. Stephen Hawking - The Quiet Luminary Of The Cosmos   171

31. Swami Vivekananda - The Quiet Catalyst Of Global Spiritual Awakening   175

32. Osho - The Quiet Revolutionary Of Inner Freedom   179

33. Amitabh Bachchan - The Quiet Titan Of Indian Cinema   183

34. Ratan Tata - The Quiet Architect Of A Legacy   187

***

***

***

***

***

The End   201

About the Author   203

Share Your Thoughts with me!   205

Success is often portrayed as a dazzling spotlight, a stage adorned with applause, and a booming voice declaring triumph. But for someone like me—an introvert—success is not a single, grand moment. It is a mosaic of quiet perseverance, and small victories accumulated over time.

Growing up, I often felt like the world was too loud and fast for someone like me. Classrooms buzzed with chatter, playgrounds echoed with shouts, and the louder you were, the more you seemed to matter. I was the child in the corner with a book, the teenager who found solace in a journal rather than a party, and the adult who dreaded networking events with their sea of superficial conversations. Society's unspoken rule—that success belongs to those who speak up, stand out, and shine bright—left me doubting whether someone like me could ever make it.

As a child, My quiet nature was frequently misunderstood as shyness or a lack of confidence. But in those silent moments, I felt an inexplicable pull—an invitation to look inward. Solitude became my sanctuary, a space where I could connect with the divine essence within me. At first, I didn't recognize the 'spiritual significance' of my introversion. It took years of self-doubt, external pressures, and failed attempts to conform to society's expectations before I realized that my quietness was a 'gift', not a flaw. It was in silence that I learned to listen—not just to others, but to the whisper of the divine guiding me toward my purpose.

The path was not without struggle. There were moments when the world's noise drowned out that 'sacred whisper'. I fought battles with self-doubt, questioning whether someone like me, who thrived in stillness, could ever succeed in a world designed for the bold and outspoken. But each challenge became an opportunity for spiritual growth.

Through prayer, meditation, and moments of deep introspection, I began to see myself not as inadequate, but as divinely crafted for a unique purpose. I learned that my ability to reflect deeply, to create space for others, and to connect with the unseen was not only valuable but sacred. My introversion became a bridge to the divine—a pathway to understanding the interconnectedness of all things and the quiet strength that flows through us all. The subtle string of cosmic energy that binds us all as one.

Today, as I reflect on my journey, I see how every struggle and triumph was a step towards my 'journey to universal wisdom'. My success is not about standing out in a crowd; it is about standing firm in my truth. It is about using my 'quiet nature' to bring peace, to serve others, to create meaning, and to inspire those who, like me, have felt out of place in a noisy world.

To my fellow introverts, I want to share this:

Your quietness is not a limitation; it is an invitation to discover the sacred depths within you. Embrace the stillness, for it is in those moments of solitude that you will find your strength, your purpose, and your connection to the divine. Do not be discouraged if the world doesn't always understand you. The most profound truths are often spoken softly.

Know that your journey, however unique, has immense value. Success is not about changing who you are to fit the world—it is about being true to yourself and letting your quiet light shine. Trust your path, however unconventional it may seem. You were not made to follow the noise; you were made to create harmony.

You have a gift the world needs: the ability to see beyond the surface, to feel deeply, and to bring wisdom from the quiet corners of your soul.

> *"Step forward, not with noise, but with purpose. Let your quiet strength change the world in ways 'only you can"*

PROLOGUE

'*Spiritual awakening*' is a transformative journey that many people yearn for, but its path varies greatly depending on one's personality and life circumstances. Intriguingly, introverts often find themselves more naturally attuned to the process of spiritual awakening than their extroverted counterparts. This tendency is not merely coincidental; it stems from the inherent characteristics of introversion that align seamlessly with the requirements of 'spiritual exploration' and 'inner transformation'.

At its core, spiritual awakening demands soul searching—a deep dive into one's inner world to uncover truths that often lie buried beneath layers of societal conditioning and external distractions. Introverts, by nature, are inclined toward introspection. They derive energy from solitude and often prioritize reflective activities over external stimulation. This natural fondness for turning inward creates fertile ground for the seeds of spiritual awakening to take root.

One of the hallmarks of spiritual awakening is the capacity to sit with 'silence'. Silence is not merely the absence of sound; it is a state of being where one can connect with the subtle vibrations of existence. For many extroverts, silence can feel daunting or even oppressive, as they thrive in environments rich with social interaction and external stimuli. Introverts, however, often find solace in silence. Their comfort with being alone allows them to embrace moments of stillness, where profound spiritual insights often arise. In this state, they can tune into the whispers of intuition and the deeper layers of consciousness that are pivotal for spiritual growth.

Another reason spiritual awakening comes more easily to introverts is their tendency to process experiences 'deeply'. While extroverts may focus on immediate reactions and external validation, introverts often take the time to analyze and internalize their experiences. This deep processing enables introverts to identify patterns, question assumptions, and seek meaning in life events—the key aspects of a spiritual journey.

Moreover, introverts are less likely to be swayed by the 'cacophony' of societal expectations. They often operate independently of the mainstream, preferring authenticity over conformity. This resistance to external pressures makes it easier for introverts to pursue a path that may seem 'unconventional' to most, such as spiritual awakening. Free from the need to constantly engage with others or seek approval, introverts can dedicate their energy to exploring their spiritual inclinations without fear of judgment.

The practice of mindfulness and meditation—two essential tools for spiritual awakening—also comes naturally to introverts. Both practices require the ability to focus inward and sustain attention over time, skills that introverts often excel at. While extroverts may struggle to quiet their minds or sit still for prolonged periods, introverts are more accustomed to this inward focus. Their affinity for solitude becomes an asset, allowing them to delve deeper into meditative states and connect with the transcendent aspects of existence.

We introverts often possess a heightened sensitivity to the 'unseen and intangible'. This sensitivity, which may manifest as an acute awareness of energy, emotions, or subtle shifts in the environment, aligns closely with spiritual experiences on earth. Many spiritual traditions emphasize the importance of attuning to subtleness of existence, and introverts are naturally predisposed to such attunement. If you are an introvert and cannot miss a 'tiny detail', you know what I mean. This quality not only enhances the mindfulness of our daily lives if channelized correctly, but also creates a deeper connection with the divine or universal consciousness.

Now please don't get me wrong. I don't intend to suggest that extroverts cannot attain spiritual awakening; they simply navigate a different path. For extroverts, the journey may involve balancing their outward focus with intentional inward exploration. But most introverts often find that their 'natural tendencies' already align effortlessly with the demands of spiritual awakening.

"By embracing their true nature, seeking solitude, and tuning into their inner world, introverts unlock doors to spiritual realms with a sense of ease and grace."

ACKNOWLEDGEMENTS

I would like to thank my family for being there for me in tough times and through their actions, setting an example of what hardwork and dedication must look like. To watch them carry on with their lives in spite of disappointments gave birth to a drive in me.

The drive to grow into the best version of myself even if it wasn't in the most predictable way.

Theres still a long journey to make but I believe what is planted right, will begin with half the work done, just like in my case.

Writing *The Divine Significance of Being an Introvert* has been an enriching journey, and I owe my deepest gratitude to several remarkable individuals whose contributions for the world have impacted my understanding and perspective on introversion.

First and foremost, I am profoundly grateful to Albert Einstein, whose revolutionary ideas and deep contemplations remind us of the power of introspection and the beauty of a thoughtful, introspective mind.

To Marie Curie, whose groundbreaking work in science and her unwavering dedication serve as a beacon of perseverance and intellectual curiosity, I extend my heartfelt thanks. Her achievements highlight the profound impact of introspective study and quiet determination.

J.K. Rowling has inspired countless readers and writers alike with her imaginative storytelling and resilience. Her ability to create worlds through introspective reflection is a testament to the power of inner thoughts and creativity.

My sincere appreciation goes to Bill Gates, whose insights into technology and philanthropy reflect the importance of thoughtful analysis and strategic thinking, qualities often nurtured by introspection.

Stephen Hawking has left an indelible mark on our understanding of the universe. His ability to explore complex concepts while confronting personal challenges exemplifies the strength and depth of the introverted mind.

Swami Vivekananda's profound teachings on self-awareness and inner strength resonate deeply with the themes of this book. His wisdom provides a timeless perspective on the significance of introspection.

I am also thankful to Osho for his insights into meditation and self-discovery. His work has illuminated the path of self-awareness and the profound impact of embracing one's inner world.

Amitabh Bachchan, whose extraordinary career and reflective nature embody the spirit of perseverance and introspection, has been a source of inspiration for me. His journey underscores the significance of inner reflection in achieving greatness.

Finally, Ratan Tata's commitment to social causes and thoughtful leadership exemplify the impact of a reflective and considerate approach to making a difference in the world. His contributions remind us of the value of introspective leadership.

Each of these individuals has, in their own way, illuminated the path of understanding and embracing the introverted self.

With deep gratitude,
Paromita Ganguli

Part 1

I

Myths Vs Reality

So let us start by busting some popular myths about introverts:

1. Introverts are Shy: While some introverts may be shy, introversion itself is not synonymous with 'shyness'. Introversion refers to how individuals gain energy—through inward reflection and solitude—rather than through social interactions like extroverts. Why is it so hard to understand?

2. Introverts Dislike People: This myth suggests that introverts are antisocial or don't enjoy the company of others. In reality, introverts usually have deep long lasting relationships but may prefer smaller, more intimate gatherings over large social events. They just follow the concept of quality over quantity.

&

3. Introverts are Unfriendly or Aloof: Because introverts may not always initiate conversations or participate in small talk, they are sometimes misunderstood as being unfriendly. In truth, introverts often prefer meaningful conversations and therefore take time to warm up in social situations.

&

4. Introverts Can't Lead: There's a misconception that introverts lack leadership qualities because they may not be as outspoken or assertive in groups. However, those who believe for that to be true should be surprised that many successful leaders in real life identify as introverts and excel in leadership roles by leveraging their hardcore listening skills, clarity of mind, unconditional thoughtfulness, and impeccable focus.

&

5. Introverts Always Want to Be Alone: While introverts do recharge their energy through solitude, they also appreciate and enjoy social interactions—especially those that are deep and aligned with their interests. They simply need more downtime to recover from the clutter of unwanted energy coming from social engagements.

&

6. Introverts Are Not Team Players: Contrary to this myth, introverts can be highly effective team players. They often contribute by going the extra mile, offering thoughtful insights, and working well in situations where they can make significant contributions.

7. Introversion Can Be Changed: How many times in your life have you witnessed People trying to 'Change' Introverts? Introversion is a natural personality trait that remains relatively stable throughout life. It is not something that can or needs to be 'fixed'. While introverts can adapt and develop different social skills if they wish to, this has to be understood and accepted that their preference for solitude is a 'core' aspect of their identity.

Understanding these myths helps to recognize and appreciate the unique strengths and characteristics that introverts bring to various aspects of life, including relationships, work environments, and personal growth.

***

Not all those who are silent are lost. Some are listening to the divine whisper of the universe.

II

The Dunning-Kruger Effect: An Interesting Glimpse into the Human Mind

"Still waters run deep. The quiet ones have the most powerful ripples."
— Anonymous

Where does true 'confidence' come from? From knowing more or being more intelligent right? That was the usual assumption while growing up for me as well due to always being surrounded by people who never looked insecure or unsure of anything even when they were wrong. I saw them in a high light thinking I lack this amazing quality.

And then one day, through my love for research, I read about the Dunning-Kruger effect and my mind was completely blown. Coined by psychologists David Dunning and Justin Kruger in 1999, the Dunning-Kruger Effect reveals a profound irony. It says - Those who lack competence in a domain often 'overestimate' their abilities, blissfully unaware of their shortcomings. Conversely, those who really excel in something tend to underestimate their expertise, assuming that what comes easily to them must be simple for others. This duality— 'overconfidence' born from 'ignorance' and 'self-doubt' rooted in 'mastery'—paints a very interesting picture of the human mind.

For example, imagine a beginner in chess who has learned the basic moves. They might think, "I'm really good at this game! I could probably beat experienced players." They don't yet know how complex chess strategies can be. Meanwhile, an experienced chess player might say, "I'm okay, but there's still so much to learn." They are aware of the 'depth and nuances' of the game. This mismatch happens because beginners usually don't know enough to even recognize what they don't know, while experts understand the 'vastness' of the subject.

Similarly, an extrovert might say, "I'm great at conversations; everyone loves talking to me!" even if they dominate discussions and don't give others a chance to speak. Whereas, an introvert might think, "I'm terrible at socializing," even though others appreciate their meaningful and considerate approach to conversations. How eye opening is that?

A more cognitive understanding of the 'vastness' and 'connection' of human experience often leads some people to be very mindful of every step they take in life. Such as, I would not in my wildest dreams just walk up to someone and say - "hey you loud people, don't you have something useful to do?" because I understand that there are different kinds of people in the world and everyone has the right to be themselves harmlessly. But to my surprise, many extroverts have found it easy to throw it on my face like - "What are you doing! Come out of your shell, why are you 'antisocial'? don't be 'shy', we are not monsters haha" While I was just comfortably reading a book in the corner. What gave them the AUDACITY? How can people who make life difficult for others ever be celebrated as more 'confident' and 'outgoing'? How can lack of wisdom and empathy be placed on a pedestal?

According to me, true confidence should stem from the 'pride' of being a righteous human being. To be a reliable, safe and trustworthy force in a world full of people who are up to no good. People who are the reason for 'faith' in humanity to still exist should fill up their minds with self-worth and walk with their heads held high. Because..that just makes logical and spiritual sense.

***

**Blessed are those who see beautiful things
in humble places where others see nothing.**

III

Sacred Solitude: The Spiritual Concept of Isolation

Solitude, in a modern and every setting, is often misunderstood as mere isolation or loneliness. It is shown as something sad in the mainstream. But in the spiritual context, it holds profound significance. It is not about the absence of others, but rather the presence of oneself and, often, the divine. Spiritual solitude is a deliberate practice, a retreat into the quiet spaces of the heart and mind where one can connect deeply with the inner self and the transcendent.

In many spiritual traditions, solitude is seen as a path to self-discovery and enlightenment. *From the hermits of Christianity and the wandering monks of Buddhism to the ascetics of Hinduism and the Sufi mystics of Islam, the act of withdrawing from the world has been regarded as a way to access higher truths.* These traditions teach that the noise of daily life can obscure our connection to the divine, and solitude offers a sanctuary where clarity and insight can emerge.

One of the key aspects of spiritual solitude is the opportunity it provides for extreme focus. In solitude, distractions fade, and one is confronted with the raw truth of their thoughts, emotions, and desires. This confrontation can be uncomfortable, as it strips away the masks we wear in social settings. However, it is also liberating, as it allows us to face our authentic selves. Through this process, we can identify patterns, heal wounds, and cultivate a deeper understanding of our purpose and values.

Moreover, solitude creates a space for communion with the supreme power. Whether one believes in God, a universal energy, or the inner spirit, solitude offers a channel for dialogue with this greater presence. *In the silence, prayers can be more heartfelt, meditations more profound, and insights more illuminating.* The sacred texts of various religions often recount instances where solitude led to divine revelations—Moses on Mount Sinai, Jesus in the wilderness, Muhammad in the Cave of Hira, and the Buddha under the Bodhi tree. These moments highlight the transformative power of withdrawing from the world to seek spiritual wisdom.

However, spiritual solitude is not about permanent withdrawal. It is a practice meant to enhance our engagement with the world. By stepping back and gaining perspective, we can return to our communities with greater compassion, clarity, and resilience. Solitude teaches us to be present and attentive, qualities that enrich our relationships and interactions. It is a reminder that true connection with others begins with a deep connection to ourselves.

In modern times, the practice of spiritual solitude has become more challenging yet more necessary. The constant barrage of information, the demands of work, and the pull of social media can leave little room for quiet reflection. Yet, carving out moments of solitude—whether through a walk in nature, a silent retreat, or simply sitting in stillness—can be profoundly grounding. It allows us to tune out the external noise and listen to the whispers of our soul.

In conclusion, the spiritual concept of solitude is a journey inward, a practice of seeking truth and transcendence in the stillness. It is not an escape from life but a deeper immersion into its essence. Through solitude, we discover who we are, strengthen our connection to the divine, and emerge better equipped to navigate the complexities of the world. It is a sacred practice that reminds us that within the silence lies the voice of wisdom, guiding us toward a life of purpose and peace.

Why 'Wisdom' Flourishes in Solitude and the Unique Insight of Introverts:

Wisdom often flourishes in solitude because it is in these quiet moments that the mind is free to ponder, reflect, and grow. This process of introspection is essential for developing wisdom, as it allows individuals to analyze their experiences, draw meaningful conclusions, and gain a clearer understanding of the world and their place within it.

For introverts, who naturally gravitate toward introspection and solitude, this process is amplified. they often find their energy in quiet and contemplative environments, where they can explore their thoughts without interruption. This affinity for solitude provides them with ample opportunities to process information deeply, identify patterns, and consider multiple perspectives. As a result, many introverts exhibit a maturity and insight that can seem beyond their years.

Another factor that contributes to the wisdom of introverts is their preference for 'listening' over speaking. In social settings, introverts are often observers, absorbing details and nuances that others may overlook. This attentive nature allows them to learn from the experiences and behaviors of others, enriching their understanding of human nature and relationships. Introverts are also less likely to act impulsively, as they tend to carefully weigh their options and consider long-term consequences, further adding to their reputation for wisdom.

It is important to note that the wisdom derived from solitude and introspection is not exclusive to introverts. Extroverts can also benefit from moments of quiet reflection, even if they require more effort to step away from their social engagements. Ultimately, wisdom is a product of intentionality—the deliberate choice to pause, reflect, and seek understanding, whether one is naturally introverted or extroverted.

In a world that often prioritizes constant activity and external validation, the quiet wisdom of solitude is a reminder of the power of stillness. It teaches us that some of the most profound insights come not from the noise of the crowd but from the silence within. Whether through the natural tendencies of introverts or the deliberate practice of solitude by anyone, wisdom thrives in the spaces where the mind and soul are free to explore, unencumbered by the distractions of daily life.

***

Quiet people have the loudest minds.

IV

Protection from Low Vibrational Energies

Energy is everywhere. Where is it not? Everything in the universe - tangible or intangible, vibrates at a certain frequency. This piece of information is not a secret anymore. But back then, when I was a kid in the early 2000s, no such concept was ever spoken about and everything seemed surface level. Theoretical. By the book.

Something 'different' was just - weird. 'Uniqueness' was far from being celebrated and most people like me who had vivid and imaginative minds struggled with feeling comfortable in their own skin.

As a result of which, I felt like a terrible loser for not being able to make connections instantly like others. I remember looking at myself in the mirror with tears in my eyes. I tried so hard to hide my real personality and squeeze myself into what would look so called 'normal'. And then over the years, I gathered a 'fear of being seen'. At school/college, most of the time I never raised my hand even when I knew the answer perfectly well. When I had a doubt, 'googling' about it felt safer than being vulnerable in class. I could not even voice my opinion on what game I thought we should play because what if that was different from everyone else's choice?

Fast forward to the times when I'm writing this book. There are so many things I've learnt and one of the most profound ones is - I was saved from so many heartbreaks, politics, and petty circumstances only because I kept to myself. I never entered the world of unnecessary 'drama' and instead kept my life devoid of what I like to call 'ENERGY LEAKS'.

Were all those people that I felt like I should be connected with, really worth it? What would they have really added to my life? My closest friends may have been few in number but they have stood with me through thick and thin. Time spent with them is always emotionally fulfilling. What more could I have wanted in life?

Did the divine not keep me away from spending my precious energy on just about everything and everyone to bless me profoundly?

Is that not the reason why I'm not a distracted Individual and have mental and spiritual clarity?

Is that not the reason for why I am sharing my knowledge to empower people like me and adding value to the world?

Of Course a visionary mindset can never belong with people who aren't open in the mind space. No words are needed for that. The 'disparity' in both energies is so evident that they never feel truly resonant.

There is so much liberation in realizing the truth and completely surrendering to what was meant to be originally made of me. As I sit in my room comfortable in my own company, it feels empowering to share my insights with all you amazing readers.

Everything in the universe is so random and yet surprisingly just as it should be. Who weaves the cloth of existence to tailor every corner just right? Why do the dots always connect when looked backwards?

By the way, I've worked a lot on my fear of being seen more and more as I was brought more in touch with the divine consciousness. There is so much strength in seeing yourself as one of divine's graceful creations. Because what is more beautiful than a mind that is aware and awake with almost no 'clutter' of unnecessary energies?

That is when I connected my dots and realized that so many amazing people in the world have, in fact, identified as 'black sheeps' or 'introverts' early in their lives. Being one myself, I totally understand where it comes from. 'The awareness' that we are capable and therefore should contribute something for the betterment of the world in some way to help it make a better place, is not for the faint hearted. And it finds us at the right time. It knows we are the one's crafted differently.

Guess what? Even being a genuine human being and operating on compassion in today's day and age is of great service to the world and to the divine.

Dear Reader, please see the light in you and know that the world is still livable because of people who refuse to give up and don't turn to treacherous ways :)

***

The quieter you are, the more you can hear.

V
Creation of a Beast-Mindset

The first time I came across the word 'Beast Mode' was through instagram. The arrival of reels and shorts have affected our reality way beyond what could have been expected before. Does anyone spend a day without scrolling through them anymore? one day I saw a reel with a war-cry like background music saying:

How to activate 'beast mode' and become invincible:

1. Set Your Target

* Know exactly what you want to achieve.
    * Say it out loud: "This is what I'm going to crush today!"

2. Eliminate Distractions

* Put your phone on silent, clear your space, limit socializing and focus on the task.

3. Hype Yourself Up

* Blast some energetic music or watch a quick motivational video.
    * Repeat: "I've got this. Let's go!"

4. Go All In

* *Start strong, push hard, and don't stop until you're done.*

* Ignore doubts—just keep moving forward.

5. Stay Consistent

* Repeat every day until it becomes a habit.

6. Track and Reflect

* Monitor your progress and celebrate milestones.

   * Reflect on what worked and what didn't to adjust your approach.

‽

HOLD ON. I have lived in 'beast' mode all my life?! All that society tries to stop people from doing by calling them 'nerds' is actually the code to long term success? And here I was, hiding my passion, writing about my goals and to do lists in secret, subscribing to the norm of 'trying to look cool and easy'.

But thank god, I was a tough nut to crack while growing up. Even if I couldn't voice my opinions outwardly, I still held on tightly to the things I loved the most. No one could take that away from me. My parents used to sometimes have a hard time trying to discipline a little girl who had a mind of her own. But as years passed and they saw it in me, the grit and strong self-belief, they started trusting me more. And for that I'm truly grateful to them.

People after getting into the daily grind such as the nine to five, tend to lose out on what their heart wants due to the lack of time, energy and 'grit'.

‽

Research indicates that a significant number of individuals do not pursue their childhood dreams into adulthood. For instance, a survey found that only 14% of American adults are working in their childhood dream jobs, meaning 86% did not achieve these early aspirations. Additionally, many people set goals but struggle to achieve them. Studies show that while only 20% of individuals set long term goals, 70% of them do not reach these objectives. These findings suggest that a considerable portion of the population either shifts away from their initial goals or faces challenges in accomplishing them as they grow older. And yet, there are some people who manage to get it done. An article on Medium claims that 98% of billionaires are introverts, citing examples like Bill Gates, Warren Buffett, and Elon Musk. Interesting?

Have you noticed that the most influential and successful people in the world don't just 'print' money. They provide something substantial to the society. How does that happen?

Impact Consciousness + Beast Mindset = The most powerful souls on earth.

Every introvert or misfit, is full of insecurities and faces challenges early on in life. But the moment they finally crack open, is when magic happens. The overall aura of a person transforms completely into a beautiful magnetic energy field. That is the power of accepting the divine significance of being created a certain way.

The creation of a beast mindset is quite a journey. A path that is uncertain and often filled with obstacles. But once a person reaches the other side and connects the dots backwards, it all makes sense. Beautifully.

***

You were born with wings; why prefer to
crawl through life?

VI
The Phoenix Method

"Introverts are like tea bags. You don't know how strong they are until you put them in hot water."
— *Anonymous*

Introverts often face a unique set of challenges and strengths when navigating the world around them. In a society that tends to value extroversion—where being loud, assertive, and outgoing is often equated with success—introverts may sometimes feel as though their quieter, more reflective nature is a disadvantage. However, introverts possess a powerful spiritual strength that, when harnessed correctly, can enable them to set an inspiring example for others. One of the most transformative ways introverts can cultivate their inner power is by utilizing the Phoenix Method, a conceptual approach to personal transformation that draws on themes of rebirth, resilience, and spiritual awakening.

The Introverted Spirit: A Source of Inner Power

Introverts often thrive in solitude, finding comfort in reflection, deep thought, and connection with their inner world. While this may seem like a disadvantage in an extroverted society, it is in fact a wellspring of untapped spiritual energy. Introverts have the ability to cultivate inner peace, deepen self-awareness, and attune to their intuition in ways that others may struggle to do. Their introspective nature allows them to connect with higher consciousness, understand the subtleties of emotions, and develop a profound understanding of the world around them.

Introverts possess the spiritual power of quiet resilience. Their journey may be one of patience, introspection, and inner strength, and when they learn to embrace and share this gift with the world, they become powerful examples of transformation. It is through the Phoenix Method that introverts can rise to their full potential.

The Phoenix Method: Rebirth and Transformation

The Phoenix Method is rooted in the symbolic idea of the Phoenix, a mythical bird that is reborn from its own ashes. This symbol of regeneration is an apt metaphor for the introverted journey of self-discovery. Just as the Phoenix goes through a cycle of destruction and renewal, introverts can experience moments of personal crisis, only to emerge stronger and more enlightened than before.

For introverts, the Phoenix Method involves recognizing moments of inner struggle, challenge, or burnout as opportunities for growth. Instead of seeing themselves as weak or broken, introverts can reframe these periods as times of necessary transformation. By embracing change and shedding old patterns or limiting beliefs, they allow themselves to be reborn in a new and more powerful form.

There are several key principles of the Phoenix Method that introverts can use to harness their spiritual powers:

Self-Awareness and Reflection: The first step is to acknowledge the need for transformation. This requires a deep level of introspection, allowing the introvert to see where they may be holding themselves back or where they may need to evolve. Through practices such as meditation, journaling, or mindfulness, introverts can connect with their inner wisdom and understand the root of their challenges.

Embracing Vulnerability: The process of rebirth often involves vulnerability, which can be uncomfortable for introverts who are naturally private. However, embracing vulnerability allows introverts to open themselves up to growth and change. This vulnerability might manifest in personal relationships, work, or public speaking—areas where introverts traditionally shy away. By allowing themselves to be vulnerable, introverts can set an example of courage and authenticity for others.

Transformation Through Action: The Phoenix does not remain in its ashes forever; it rises through action. For introverts, this means taking deliberate, small steps toward their goals, even if it feels uncomfortable. By pursuing their passions, sharing their knowledge, or standing up for their beliefs, introverts can embody the power of transformation. Their example becomes one of quiet strength and determination.

Rising from Adversity: As introverts often experience moments of self-doubt, social anxiety, or isolation, these challenges can be seen as the ashes from which they rise. Instead of succumbing to these feelings, introverts can use them as fuel to propel themselves forward. The Phoenix Method teaches that adversity is not a sign of defeat but an opportunity for growth, enabling introverts to build resilience and inspire others who are facing similar struggles.

Setting an Example for the World

The true power of introverts lies in their ability to be deeply authentic and spiritually grounded. By embracing the Phoenix Method, introverts can step into their full potential and lead with quiet strength. Rather than conforming to societal expectations of extroversion, they can offer a refreshing alternative by leading with humility, insight, and compassion.

Introverts who use the Phoenix Method as a guiding principle become role models for others, showing that it is possible to achieve greatness through inner strength rather than outward display. By overcoming their own inner struggles, they become shining examples of how spiritual power can be used to transform both oneself and the world around them.

These introverted leaders do not seek attention or praise, but their actions speak volumes. They set an example of living authentically, cultivating self-awareness, and embracing the cycles of growth and renewal. In doing so, they inspire others—both introverts and extroverts alike—to tap into their own spiritual power and rise from their challenges, just as the Phoenix does.

So what are you waiting for?

***

Who looks outside, dreams; but who looks
inside, awakens.

VII
Success for introverts

"Introverts may not always seek the spotlight, but their strength shines through in their thoughtful actions and profound insights."
— Unknown

So what does success look like? Authority? Fame? Money? Assets?

The meaning goes beyond mere accomplishments. It encompasses fulfillment, satisfaction, and often involves a sense of 'progression or improvement' in one's everyday life. I have come across many introverts who struggle in truly embodying 'success'. I believe it has to do a lot with the mainstream idea of success and 'cliche' ways of pursuing it. I mean it. All my life I've heard that in order to be successful, one needs to 'work really hard', 'be flexible to life's circumstances', 'Adapt with the latest trends' etc.

While I agree with all that, there is something missing.

Let me explain to you what that is.

Do you relate with straining your eyes and yawning all day long, fantasizing about the weekend and looking at the watch over and over again, waiting to leave work? after being in the energy of 'running away' all day long, and sharing reels about 'corporate slavery' what do you think is getting embedded in your subconscious mind and eventually to your life?

Please understand that if you want to be successful, 'hard work' with a headache will never create anything worthwhile. Ever. The only way to be truly successful is to 'PUT YOUR HEART AND SOUL INTO SOMETHING'. Only when your work causes you to lose track of time, take away your sleep and yet fill you with energy instead of lethargy, you know that; it is your soul that is satisfied. You feel like the world is your oyster and you are the master of your fate. And that is when the real magic happens. When no amount of work feels 'hard' and you don't picture escape scenarios.

When all you can think about is immersing the whole of your being into whatever you do. When taking a 'break' means staying away from your passion.

When I sit to write, I absolutely get lost. I write and write and write and can go on for hours without getting distracted by anything. The only thing that can stop me is Maa being concerned and ranting about me not moving for hours and if everything is alright. And that used to happen only when I went to play outside as a child. I enjoyed a little too much without any track of time and Maa would come scolding. That feeling was the best in the world.

I say why can't life be the same child's play forever?

So while I've made it clear about what true success means,

coming back to what is in it for introverts to understand.

- How do you feel working in a really fast paced environment where 'feelings' are obsolete?
- How do you feel while chasing targets everyday that 'mean nothing to you'?
- Do you value being 'sleek' over doing the 'right thing'?
- Do you value collective growth or just climbing a so-called 'ladder' at a place that can replace you in a matter of days?
- Do you value instant gratification or long term happiness?

I am not trying to criticize any kind of work or profession. I am trying to remind you of the fact that you should be 'aware' if most of what you do everyday is taking you far away from 'who you really are'.

Everything in life takes work. Why not accumulate your energy towards things that make more sense to you? why not understand what your 'best skills are' and then capitalize on them? ask yourself today. What is it that I would love to do everyday even for free!

What am I known for usually? What comes naturally to my personality? what has the universe originally crafted me for?

Your immediate reaction would be - that looks easy in theory. What if I like to sit in a secluded place and paint? should I leave my job and start painting? will that earn me more money that what I currently have?

I say you're right. When I first thought of the same, it was terrifying. But let me ask you something. Don't you know that paintings are bought by the right people who appreciate it for any price under the sun? Taking your art to that level and scaling your shop to the right audience may be difficult but those who have reached there also needed to 'start' somewhere right?

Have you come accross 'Art Channels' on youtube? They make money from just the amount of 'views' they get for their art. Also some of them 'teach' how to draw or paint.

And how about Art classes? Can be done online or offline!

There are so many different ways to pursue what you want the only condition being the 'courage' to start.

Don't think of being the best 'Artist of India' earning lakhs of money for now creating unnecessary anxiety. Just think of making time mandatorily for something you 'love' during the weekends. And eventually let it flow in the right direction.

Look at me for instance. I have been at a full time job for more than three years now. Different challenges pulled my attention at times but I have still managed to do what my heart calls out for. I make time after work and on the weekends to write about all that I know so that I can be of some help to the society because that is what I want from life. I have always wanted to 'be of service' in some way.

And that is how you are holding my book. I did not start out thinking of being the best writer ever. And yet my achievement here is that having a full time job did not stop me from being a 'Published Author.' From sharing my opinions. From helping my people. From being me. And that makes me the happiest!

From the above given examples, please take whatever resonates with your life. I would love to one day hear stories of you picking yourself up, walking in the direction of what fulfills you and eventually getting rewarded for the same.

"Align with your soul's energy in anything you do and there will be no looking back."

***

The biggest privilege of a lifetime is to
become who you truly are.

VIII

Soul Connections: The Only Relationships We Need

"Quiet influence is often the most impactful, as it comes from a place of genuine connection and understanding."
— Anonymous

Despite the stereotype that successful careers require extroverted qualities like charisma and assertiveness, introverts can leverage their innate traits to excel, particularly by nurturing deep connections with a select few. Introverts tend to excel in one-on-one interactions, where they can fully engage and listen attentively. These traits are invaluable in building strong, trusting relationships with colleagues, mentors, and clients. By focusing on quality over quantity in their relationships, introverts can cultivate networks based on mutual respect and genuine understanding.

These connections often yield valuable insights, opportunities for collaboration, and support during challenging times in their career journey. Since introverts often prefer to reflect deeply on their experiences and insights, 'close relationships' can serve as sounding boards for their ideas, allowing them to refine their thoughts and develop innovative solutions to challenges in their careers. Therefore, do not fret when things don't go in your career as smoothly as you want. Just try to leverage your best qualities, such as building 'one to one' meaningful and strong relationships that help you combat many other challenges.

Throughout my life, I haven't hung out with 'twenty' people at once. Just because I don't enjoy it. But does that mean I've lost out on opportunities? Or that I've suffered alone? Not at all. Because the 'four' people that I made close relationships with, were way more concerned and giving towards me (less quantity, more quality). When I was desperately in search of a job, they went out of their way to 'create' an opportunity for me. When I felt like going nowhere, It was safe to be at their place. Ironically, most people - Even extroverts at a certain age realize the truth of life that not everyone that laughs with you is your 'friend'. Just acquaintances. It's just that being an introvert I always sensed that and naturally lost out on one thing - Unnecessary drama and meaningless pursuits. Saved my energy and focused on things that matter. And what truly matters to me? Working on myself everyday. I'm an endless project in my eyes. Just like I've come a long way from where I started, I intend to go miles before I sleep forever.

If you come to think of me as someone useful in any way, know that it is due to the strength of those 'few meaningful relationships that I have in life'.

Therefore, understand the divine blessing of the ability to spot a diamond in the coalmine. And make the best use of your relationship building skills. They will take you places.

Use your quality oriented choices to make the most of your few meaningful relationships in any area of your life. You will soon realize that nothing more was ever needed. It was just the societal pressure that made you feel like you're missing out.

People who love us genuinely stand by our side no matter what and it is a truly heart warming experience, sharing our live's experiences with them.

So, I may not be the best networker or marketer out there, but I believe in my divinely gifted strengths and follow my heart when it comes to almost everything. And in some way or the other, it works out. Always.

The people who believe in good and live with their soul find me. Or I find them. Always. And that ois enough for me to fulfill my heart's will and my soul's purpose.

Just like an amazing person - YOU picked up my book. Thank you so much :)

***

You cannot always control what goes on
outside, but you can always control what
goes on inside.

IX

Awareness: The Bulletproof Mindset

"Introverts possess a unique creative power: the ability to turn quiet moments into masterpieces and introspective thoughts into brilliant ideas." — Anonymous

Imagine you're stuck in traffic on your way to an important meeting. Frustration builds as the minutes tick by, and your mind races with worries about being late and the potential consequences. In this moment, the problem feels overwhelming, and your emotional reaction amplifies it. Now, let's introduce awareness into the situation. Instead of getting caught up in the frustration and fear, you take a deep breath and bring your attention to the present moment. You notice the tension in your shoulders and consciously relax them. You observe the sound of the car engine, the rhythm of your breathing, and the play of light on the cars around you. As you do this, the frantic thoughts about the meeting begin to lose their grip. And with that, You realize that arriving late isn't the end of the world. And then focus on how to handle it gracefully.

With awareness, you recognize that while you can't control the traffic, you can control your response to it. The problem hasn't changed—you're still in traffic—but it no longer feels as consuming. Awareness has shifted your perspective, allowing you to approach the situation with calm and clarity. This simple practice shows how 'awareness' can transform a problem that feels 'big' and 'stressful' into something small and manageable. By stepping back and observing the situation without judgment, you realize that most problems are temporary and much smaller than they initially appear.

An aware mind is often regarded as the strongest mind because it possesses the capacity to navigate life with clarity, resilience, and purpose. Awareness—the ability to be fully present and observe thoughts, emotions, and experiences without judgment—is the foundation of mental strength. It empowers individuals to make deliberate choices, overcome challenges, and cultivate inner peace.

Introverts often spend considerable time reflecting on their thoughts and emotions. They find comfort and growth in solitude, which provides the ideal setting for self-awareness to flourish. This habit of introspection enables introverts to understand their feelings, identify patterns in their behavior, and develop a clear sense of self. For example, when they are faced with a difficult decision, an introvert might retreat to a quiet space, analyze the pros and cons, and tune into their emotional responses. This reflective process helps them make better decisions in life most of the time and eventually impact their surroundings positively.

As an introverted child, I often found myself in situations all by myself and as a result had no choice but to sit with my problems alone. Back then it did feel like a burden and spiked depressive thoughts. The only two choices I had was to either 'overthink' and complicate my life further or to sit with my thoughts and carefully understand them. Observe them. Learn to navigate through them. To find inspiration through positive 'self-talk'. And that gave birth to so much wisdom that I hadn't even found in books.

To this day, whenever I find myself overwhelmed, the first thing that takes over is the 'awareness' side of my mind. It almost feels like a 'mental sword' I've developed over many years as a means to protect my mind. I often find myself breathing slowly, wanting to write things down in a journal to break down the problem better and then strategize upon it. And everything instantly feels better. Becomes digestible. And People say - "You live such a sorted life. Lucky!"

***

To the mind that is still, the whole universe
surrenders.

X
The Impact Consciousness

It was a regular day in my life as a nine year old. I had just arrived from school and saw a group of 'rag-pickers' having lunch under a tree beside my garden and yapping about random things in a strange language. Seemingly uninterested in anything beyond their little world. The dustbin nearby was crammed full and apparently the best place for them to hang out. The nuances of life fascinated me. I wondered if they could even imagine the pain of failing to solve a math problem.

After some time, one of my friends arrived with her badminton kit and we went off to play. Amidst the banter of who lost a point and who won, we suddenly noticed the rag-picker kids - about the same age as us, coming close and looking intently at our game. One of the girls stood out to me the most. She had this innocent and curious smile almost wanting to ask if they could be a part of whatever we were doing.

Meanwhile my friend, without thinking twice, instantly uttered - "Look at those beggars staring at us. Hey you! Go away..shoo shoo.." It felt like a hundred needles poking me at once as I clearly saw their faces. The innocent smile immediately turned into a fierce looking rugged kid who could break a knee to avenge her own. She literally barged at us with a stick and we ran for our lives as fast as we could till they could no longer follow us. And ofcourse. My friend kept babbling about how we nearly escaped 'something risky'! And me? I was utterly disgusted with what just happened. But back then like most kids I lacked the courage to stand out. To openly express how I felt about the situation differently. Didn't say much. But the thought kept spiraling in my head again and again so I decided to apologize the next time I see them.

Yes, I became friends with a rag-picker. She often came near my house and I gave her things to eat. And she probably boasted in front of her friends about having 'connections' with posh people. The thought made me smile.

What do we learn from this story? If you ponder, things like this happen all the time where most people fail to empathize with their surroundings. nothing 'gets' to them and there is no sign of repenting either. And in the same world they coincide with others who give their lives to different causes. People who cater to stray animals. People who live sustainably. People who will not kill a fly just for the sake of it.

One of the most notable qualities in introverts lie in their deep understanding of 'impact'. Feeding a dog on the street does not just subside as an act of charity. We feel the fulfilment of being able to 'help another soul' on this planet.

Lakshmi, the rag-picker may have been one of the most insignificant people in my life but to her, I may have been the first person who showered her with unexpected compassion. I may have changed her mind into believing that not everyone we come across in life are meant to be mean. She would probably tell her children stories about how being kind can foster loving connections in society. Not everything has to be purely for 'survival'.

An experience that altered her brain chemistry. Do you think she somewhat saw 'the divine' through me?

In the vast tapestry of existence, we are all interconnected and impact each other's lives greatly. It does not have to be an extravagant gesture. Rather it is more often subtle and happens subconsciously.

If you are the only kind person at work, people will try and take advantage of that. They might even make you feel stupid for 'being nice' in today's fast-paced world. The subconscious 'collective narrative' that smart people are automatically 'cunning' and 'mean' is clearly the manifestation of devil's work

.

Then there are people who would rather be alone and alienated than lose their soul. People who would rather cry their heart out in pain than turning to sorcery. The souls that will not give into corrupt ways just because evil forces them to. The divine waits for them to realize that they have been blessed with the 'impact consciousness' as a boon for humanity.

Working as a Human Resource Professional, Being kind at work has enabled me to help people. To empower them.

To speak up for them. To be that 'one' person they can be honest and real with. To be that one person they can fully trust. Because I understand its impact on people's personal as well as professional lives in the long run.

Society isn't made of bricks and stones. It is made of 'People'. Therefore it is of utmost importance to realize our power and impact towards others. To be who we truly are with pride. Because the world was created for people like us.

Let them feel stupid for being sleek. Show them through lasting acts of kindness that it is the divine who runs the world. Let them learn that understanding 'impact consciousness' is the highest form of intelligence or smartness there can be.

***

In a gentle way, you can shake the world.

XI

Emotional Intelligence

"Introverts channel their sensitivity into a superpower that allows them to make a significant impact through their thoughtful actions and words."
— *Anonymous*

Introverts often have more activity in the 'frontal cortex' of their brain, which is associated with abstract thinking and decision-making, compared to extroverts who may have more activity in the posterior cortex, which deals with sensory and motor functions.

This results in the ability to comprehend complex situations, people or things with much ease. And then conduct themselves accordingly to make informed decisions in life that are usually fruitful in the long term.

You might recall that one person who usually keeps quiet but the best kind of advice comes from them. Or they usually seem aloof but make the best choices when it comes to their career, relationships etc.

And if that is you, congratulations on being at the higher side of the spectrum.

I want to draw your attention towards the amazing strength bestowed upon us by the universe and contemplate on the reasons for the same.

Just like throughout your life you've wondered why am I like this? It would've been so much simpler to be like 'others' who don't have to think much and everything works out pretty well for them.

I would like to remind you of the same question again. Why are you like this?

Why do you understand so much? Why does your mind make you do the right thing no matter what? Why are you always the one listening to other people's pain and offering advice or solutions? Why are you the only one rescuing or feeding animals? Why are you the only one helping the poor? Why are you always the one caring for the smallest details when others won't?

Why does it get awkward? Why can't you relate to the 'carelessness' of your surroundings?

Emotional intelligence is not to be found so easily and thats what makes it so special. You might have felt time and again that the single most reason for all your heartache lies in the fact that you 'understand' and 'care' more than others. Not surprising because I've been there too!

But the real deal is when you pass through the fogg to see what your 'understanding' and 'caring' abilities were really meant for. And that was certainly not to entertain low quality people and get stabbed in the back.

There are people who run charity organizations, animal welfare associations only to dedicate their lives towards helping the needy. They are not simply existing for the sake of appearing cool and manipulating their way to the so called 'top'.

If they are not a blessing to our planet who is?

There are people planting 'forests' and building 'eco friendly homes' when many might not even for once think before littering in a public place.

The more something is precious, the more it is rare. If you have that something in you, first be proud and then think of how it can be used for good.

***

The soul that truly sees beauty may often
walk alone.

XII

Sensitivity: The Gift of Empathy

"Introverts have a unique gift for turning silence into eloquence, using their words to express what others might only feel." — Anonymous

Most introverts seemingly have the tendency to get uncomfortable by over stimulation and are therefore found far away from places with loud noise, crowds, or even hectic environments. That may call for them to be perceived as "Hyper - sensitive". But sensitivity is not a negative but multifaceted character trait just like every other. Sure, a very sensitive individual may not appear tough on the outside but more often is a true "empath" and humanity personified.

Empathy is the ability to understand and share the feelings of another. It goes beyond mere sympathy; it involves truly resonating with someone else's emotions, experiences, and perspectives. While empathy is a quality that can be found in people of all temperaments, introverts often excel in this area due to their "reflective" nature and tendency to observe rather than dominate social interactions.

One of the defining traits of introverts is their keen observational skills. In social situations, introverts often take a step back, allowing them to absorb the nuances of human behavior. They notice body language, facial expressions, and subtle emotional cues that others may overlook. This heightened awareness enables them to understand what people are feeling, even when those feelings are unspoken.

For introverts, this observational quality is not just about gathering information; it's about connecting with the emotions behind those observations. They can often sense when someone is struggling, even if that person hasn't voiced their challenges. This ability to read the room makes introverts natural empathizers, capable of offering support and understanding in meaningful ways. They are often excellent listeners, which is a vital component of empathy. When engaged in conversation, they tend to focus intently on the speaker, providing a safe space for others to express themselves. This deep listening creates an atmosphere of trust, allowing people to open up and share their vulnerabilities.

For introverted individuals, listening is not just about hearing words; it's about connecting with the emotions behind those words. They may ask insightful questions or provide thoughtful responses that demonstrate their understanding, further deepening the connection.

Peace and calm is what calls us. Seclusion, Silence and less clutter makes us surprisingly productive and function to the best of our abilities.

But the sad part is, that most of us have been made to believe that it is some form of a shortcoming and that needs 'changing'.

This results in unnecessary pressure. The pressure to pretend. To act in ways which can draw validation from the society. To laugh even when it is not funny. To dance even when the body can't feel the rhythm. To socialize even when absolutely uninterested. To appear unfazed even when overwhelmed.

But you know what? It is never too late to acknowledge the fact clearly and precisely that we ARE sensitive.

We are sensitive to "energy" and therefore cannot expose ourselves to everything that comes across.

And the reason is not because we 'cannot' but because we aren't meant to.

Think of it this way. No change would have ever taken place in the world as no one would have stood up for the right things unless they were 'impacted' as much to give up their lives for it?

How sensitive were they? Certain issues that common people would sympathize upon, they 'empathized' with. It touched them in a way that they 'took it personally'.

Thank God, Raja Ram Mohan Roy being a man was sensitive enough to understand the pain of a woman being burnt alive in the days of 'sati' pratha.

When hundreds of people witnessed it so often, how were they able to just accept it in the name of a 'ritual'?

People may have called him names. But he did not fear being looked at as 'weak'.

We should be grateful to all the 'sensitive' people who showed up in history.

To be sensitive is a gift. A gift from the divine that is misunderstood but the most impactful when used in the right way.

It is them, who are sensitive, that often conduct themselves in the best way possible.

I have chosen to embrace the most authentic part of me and that has already created ripples. And needless to say, there may be so much more coming!

Let the divine create a difference in the world through you, chosen one.

"*Emotions have the power to create that, which is often unimaginable and quite peculiar to the logical mind.*"

***

Be the change that you wish to see in the
world.

XIII

The Subliminal Healer and Peace maker

Introverts possess an innate ability to absorb the energies of their surroundings. This sensitivity to the environment allows them to pick up on nuances that others may overlook: the slight furrow in a friend's brow, the tremor in a colleague's voice, or the unspoken tension in a room. These observations are not mere distractions; they serve as a guiding compass for how introverts engage with the world.

In chaotic situations, this strength transforms introverts into invaluable allies. When a conflict arises, their calm demeanor can diffuse tension. They can approach a heated discussion with a "thoughtful question" or a gentle reminder of shared values, steering the conversation away from confrontation and towards resolution. The ability to listen deeply and respond with empathy allows introverts to create safe spaces for dialogue, where others might only see discord.

While extroverts may thrive in the spotlight, introverts often find their strength in stillness. Their presence can be a soothing balm in times of distress. When introverts enter a chaotic space, their quiet nature tends to invite calmness. It's as if their energy stabilizes the room, offering a counterbalance to anxiety and fear.

Consider the introvert in a gathering where tensions run high: they might not be the loudest voice, but their mere presence can serve as a reminder that it's okay to slow down, to breathe, to think before reacting. Their ability to remain centered in chaos allows others to recalibrate their emotions and regain composure.

This calm presence is not passive; it is active and intentional. Introverts often employ nonverbal but very note worthy cues—soft eye contact, a gentle smile, or a reassuring nod—that communicate understanding and acceptance. In these moments, they become a *subliminal healer*, providing comfort without needing to articulate their thoughts.

From the hermits of ancient times to modern-day contemplatives, those who seek stillness are often seen as conduits of divine insight. Introverts, in their natural inclination towards reflection, embody this sacred tradition. Their healing presence is not just a personal trait;

it's a manifestation of a deeper calling, an invitation for others to connect with their own inner stillness.

The energy that introverts exude is unique. When introverts enter a room, their serene presence can shift the atmosphere. It's as if they carry an invisible shield that absorbs negativity and fosters tranquility. This ability to hold space for others is a powerful gift; it encourages vulnerability and openness, allowing individuals to confront their emotions and experiences without fear of judgment.

Introverts excel at forming meaningful connections, often preferring depth over breadth in their relationships. This inclination towards profound engagement enables them to create bonds that foster inner healing. In a world where superficial interactions dominate, introverts remind us of the "power" of authentic connection. When someone shares their struggles, introverts are there to reflect, validate, and offer comfort.

In many spiritual traditions, the act of listening is considered a form of prayer. Introverts embody this practice, holding space for others with grace and compassion. Their quiet presence serves as a reminder that we are all interconnected, that our stories are woven together in a tapestry of shared humanity.

· __The Catalyst for Peaceful Growth__

An introvert's healing presence is not just about providing comfort; it is also about catalyzing growth. By encouraging others to explore their own depths, introverts foster a sense of empowerment and resilience.

Consider the role of an introverted mentor. They may not dominate conversations, but their insights are often profound and peaceful. By sharing their experiences and encouraging others to reflect on their journeys, they calmly inspire personal growth and transformation. They remind those around them that vulnerability is a strength, that embracing one's true self can lead to authenticity.

In this way, introverts act as catalysts for change. Their gentle encouragement can ignite a spark within others, leading to a deeper understanding of oneself and a more compassionate engagement with the world.

· **The Healing Touch of Silence**

Silence is often seen as uncomfortable in a society that thrives on chatter and distraction. Yet for introverts, silence is a sacred space. It is in these moments of quiet that true healing can occur. Introverts understand that silence allows for reflection, integration, and the emergence of insights that might otherwise remain hidden.

In a world filled with noise, the introvert's ability to embrace silence is a divine gift. Their comfort in stillness invites others to explore their own relationship with silence, fostering a deeper connection to their inner selves. This exploration can lead to profound realizations, healing long-held inner child wounds, and igniting a sense of purpose.

In therapy, meditation, or even simple conversations, moments of silence can be powerful. Introverts often recognize when these pauses are necessary, using them to deepen the connection and enhance understanding.

By modeling this behavior, they subliminally teach others the importance of listening—not just to words, but to the silence in between.

***

Peace comes from within. And you seek it
out.

XIV

Self Talk: Conversations With the Divine

For many introverts, the richest conversations occur not in the company of others but within the *sanctuary of their own minds*. Isn't it interesting, to explore the art of self-talk as a means of connecting with the divine and nurturing our inner selves?

Recognizing that the divine exists within you, can be a transformative realization. For introverts, this understanding can feel particularly resonant, as it affirms the richness of their beautiful "internal world". As you engage in self-talk, remember that you are not alone; you carry the essence of the divine within you.

If you are the one with ruminating questions and doubts, then who is it that provides the clarity of path ahead? If you were able to logically form it then why did you have doubts in the first place?

Self-talk is more than just the internal chatter that runs through our minds; it is a vital dialogue that shapes our reality, influences our emotions, and connects us to something greater.

At its core, self-talk is the inner dialogue we engage in every day. It can range from mundane thoughts about what to have for breakfast to more profound reflections on our purpose and beliefs. This dialogue can be positive or negative, conscious or subconscious. The key is recognizing that this inner conversation holds power—power to uplift or diminish, empower or hinder.

Being alone allows individuals to turn inward, fostering heightened awareness of their thoughts and emotions. This self-awareness can help identify patterns, fears, and desires that may be obscured by the noise of everyday life. The divine often communicates through feelings and emotions, guiding individuals toward healing and growth. The divine can be understood as the greater consciousness that resides within us and around us. When we engage in self-talk, we are essentially opening a channel for this divine presence to communicate with us. By choosing to cultivate a mindful, intentional dialogue, we can invite inspiration and insight into our lives.

Engaging in a conversation with the divine through self talk is a journey of connection and self-discovery.

Remember, self-talk is not just an internal monologue; it is a sacred dialogue with the universe, an opportunity to explore the depths of your being. As you cultivate this practice, you'll find that the divine is not a distant entity but a vibrant part of your inner world, waiting to be acknowledged and celebrated.

If you ever encounter self-doubt, ask yourself, "What would my higher self advise?" If you're filled with joy, take a moment to express gratitude for that feeling. This ongoing conversation cultivates a sense of connection and mindfulness throughout your day.

The best kind of advice always comes often from within. The soul embodies our deepest values, desires, and truths. It is the part of us that knows our purpose and yearns for alignment with our authentic selves.

Trust is a fundamental aspect of connecting with your inner guidance. Often, we second-guess ourselves or feel compelled to seek external validation. Remind yourself that your journey is distinct. Others may have different experiences, but that doesn't diminish the value of your own insights. When faced with uncertainty, return to your inner guidance and affirm your trust in the process.

Recognizing that this kind of direction comes from the divine, the infinite source, is crucial in establishing a deep trust with one's inner self and intuition further paving way for channeling the best course of action in any situation.

The co-founder of Apple is known for his introverted personality. Wozniak has mentioned how he values time alone for self-reflection and problem-solving.

Therefore, embrace your solitary journey, trust the process, and let your conversations with the divine unfold.

***

Wise men speak because they have
something to say; fools because they have
to say something.

XV
The Age of Aquarius

"Introverts wield their words like a finely tuned instrument, using them to create resonance and impact with precision and care."
— Anonymous

So according to astrology, we are currently transitioning from the Age of 'Pisces' to the Age of 'Aquarius'. The exact timing and duration of this transition can vary depending on different astrological interpretations.

So what is the age of 'Aquarius' about? Whether you understand astrology or not, everything is deeply interconnected in the universe and it is crucial to have atleast a basic understanding of how it affects our everyday life.

This age is anticipated to bring about a focus on humanitarianism, innovation, equality, and the advancement of knowledge.

It is associated with the water bearer (Aquarius), symbolizing the dispensation of knowledge and the nurturing of collective consciousness.

You do not really have to understand astrology to get what it truly means.

Look at the world around us. Has it not transitioned drastically in the last 100 years?

Ask your grandparents what their lives looked like and compare it with gen Z.

After like thousands of years, suddenly there are questions being asked before believing blindly.

Suddenly there are discussions about 'mental well being', 'animal cruelty', 'the importance of herbalism', 'the intelligence present in ancient cultures' and what not!

People today openly speak up about subjects that were once considered taboo by the mainstream.

Also, gone are the days when it was extremely difficult to stand out from the crowd.

How many times do you come across the words 'energy' and 'universe' on social media?

Back when I was a teen, the only place I could talk about 'universe' and 'energy' was in my diary!

Practicing spirituality openly was not quite cool back then. It was still a 'taboo'.

And today, everyone has their 'individuality' in check and can get their opinions and ideas across to the world so easily!

So the point I'm trying to make is very simple. It is time for your uniqueness to shine, my dear introverts.

There was a time when I'd feel ashamed of being an introvert and now I've trasformed to write a book highlighting the spiritual connection to introversion.

In the age of aquarius, nothing is all that 'weird' any more. The vastness of the cosmos has truly unleashed and anything imaginable is possible.

The world has woken up to the fact that old beliefs and cliches won't work anymore. It is time for change. It is time for the new.

So be confident and stay in your authentic self. Whatever that may look like.

without holding back. The divine has really worked overtime in creating a safe space for everyone to finally thrive in their own ways.

You do not know how much the world needs that right now.

***

To be yourself in a world that is constantly
trying to make you something else is truly
the greatest accomplishment in life.

Part 2

XVI

Sound Healing: High Frequency Music

It is not just for superficial reasons that your mood instantly lifts or drops depending on the kind of music you listen to. Music has an exponential impact on the human psyche and is therefore used in therapy as well. Now that is a fact I'm sure you must've come across at some point in life. But most people aren't conscious about the kind of music they listen to on a daily basis. But that isn't the problem.

The point I'm trying to make is that when you can make the most of something, why not try?

As an introvert who feels deeply, you cannot imagine the impact of listening to certain high frequency music especially at the beginning of your day. For example, I love listening to 'Nirvana Shatakam' every morning on repeat for at least 15 minutes. and that takes my mind to a different realm altogether. It is almost as if I can feel the vastness of the divine and the insignificance of my problems. They seem so small.

A little world of its own inside my earphones. You can find it very easily on youtube. DO GIVE IT A TRY.

ဆာ

The Impact of Sound Therapy on the Human Body

Sound therapy, an ancient practice with roots in various cultures and traditions, has gained renewed attention in modern wellness circles. Utilizing the therapeutic power of sound to enhance physical, emotional, and mental health, sound therapy encompasses a range of techniques and instruments designed to promote healing and balance. This essay explores the multifaceted impact of sound therapy on the human body, focusing on its physiological, emotional, and cognitive effects.

• **Physiological Effects**

One of the most notable impacts of sound therapy is its effect on the body's physiological processes. Sound therapy operates on the principle that sound and vibration can influence bodily functions, promoting healing and relaxation. Different frequencies and types of sound—such as tuning forks, gongs, or singing bowls—can resonate with the body's natural vibrations, potentially leading to various health benefits.

1. *Stress Reduction:* One of the most immediate physiological effects of sound therapy is its ability to induce relaxation and reduce stress. Sound therapy often involves listening to soothing sounds or music that can activate the parasympathetic nervous system. This activation helps

lower heart rate, reduce blood pressure, and decrease cortisol levels, the hormone associated with stress. By creating a calming environment, sound therapy helps to counteract the physiological effects of chronic stress, which can contribute to numerous health issues, including cardiovascular disease and weakened immune function.

2. Pain Management: Research indicates that sound therapy can also play a role in pain management. Techniques such as vibroacoustic therapy, which involves using sound vibrations to target specific areas of the body, have been shown to reduce pain perception. The vibrations can stimulate the release of endorphins, the body's natural painkillers, and enhance circulation, which can help alleviate muscle tension and discomfort.

3. Sleep Improvement: Sound therapy has been shown to improve sleep quality, which is crucial for overall health. Gentle, calming sounds can help regulate sleep patterns and reduce insomnia by promoting relaxation and creating a conducive environment for restful sleep. Studies suggest that sound therapy can help individuals fall asleep faster and experience deeper, more restorative sleep, thereby supporting overall physical health.

₮

- **Emotional Effects**

Sound therapy's impact extends beyond the physical realm, influencing emotional well-being and psychological health. The therapeutic use of sound can help individuals process and manage emotions more effectively.

1. Emotional Release: Certain sounds and frequencies can evoke powerful emotional responses, allowing individuals to process and release pent-up emotions. This can be particularly beneficial for those dealing with trauma, grief, or emotional blockages. The cathartic effect of sound therapy can facilitate emotional healing and help individuals gain insights into their emotional states.

2. Enhanced Mood: Sound therapy has the potential to enhance mood and overall emotional well-being. Listening to music or soundscapes that are personally meaningful or soothing can trigger the release of dopamine, a neurotransmitter associated with pleasure and reward. This can lead to improved mood, increased feelings of happiness, and a greater sense of well-being.

3. Anxiety Reduction: By inducing a state of relaxation and calm, sound therapy can help reduce symptoms of anxiety. The meditative aspects of sound therapy, such as focused listening and mindfulness, can help individuals manage anxiety by shifting their attention away from stressors and promoting a sense of inner peace.

- **Cognitive Effects**

In addition to its physiological and emotional benefits, sound therapy can have a positive impact on cognitive functions.

1. Improved Focus and Concentration: Sound therapy, particularly techniques involving binaural beats or specific sound frequencies, has been associated with enhanced cognitive performance. Binaural beats, for example, can influence brainwave patterns and promote states of focus and concentration. This can be beneficial for tasks requiring mental clarity and cognitive effort.

2. Enhanced Creativity: Certain sound therapies can also stimulate creativity and problem-solving abilities. By facilitating a relaxed and open mental state, sound therapy can help individuals access creative insights and overcome mental blocks. The harmonious and rhythmic qualities of therapeutic sounds can create an environment conducive to creative thinking.

3. Memory and Learning: Emerging research suggests that sound therapy may have potential benefits for memory and learning. Some studies indicate that listening to specific types of music or sound can enhance memory retention and cognitive performance. This effect is thought to be related to the way sound influences brain function and neural connectivity.

Sound therapy offers a holistic approach to enhancing human health, with significant impacts on the physiological, emotional, and cognitive aspects of well-being. By leveraging the therapeutic power of sound and vibration, individuals can experience reduced stress, improved pain management, better sleep, and enhanced emotional and cognitive functions. As research continues to uncover the mechanisms behind sound therapy, its potential applications in promoting health and healing are likely to expand, offering new opportunities for improving quality of life and overall wellness.

There are some amazing 'soundscapes' available on youtube with soulful flute/tibetan healing bowls. These are used by millions of people in the world for sleeping, deep thinking or meditation. I personally use these while writing.

Remember, 90% of life happens in the 'mind'. Invest in keeping the beautiful mind of yours at the right place and then let the rest follow. You will see the changes through your own eyes.

Sound healing in my eyes is one of the easiest available therapy out there.

"*Through sound, we reconnect with the universal rhythm, restoring balance and peace within.*"

XVII

Use the Power of Words

Call a boy 'a gentleman' and watch his shoulders straighten.

Call a girl 'a lady' and watch her spirit turn graceful.

We tend to become what we are called. Words have impeccable power, sometimes beyond the comprehension of the third dimensional human mind.

Think about the way listening to a motivational speaker energizes you.

Think about the way a few harsh words from your Father can make you feel like nothing.

At their most potent, words wield the power to shape destinies.

They can sway nations with rhetoric, inspire movements through passionate speeches, or ignite change within the society.

In a nutshell, Using words wisely can have a profound impact in the following areas:

- **Builds Relationships:** Thoughtful words strengthen bonds and foster trust in personal and professional relationships.
- **Resolves Conflicts:** Choosing words carefully can de-escalate tensions and promote understanding in conflicts.
- **Inspires and Motivates:** Words of encouragement and positivity can uplift spirits and motivate others to achieve their goals.
- **Creates Change:** Persuasive and well-articulated words can influence opinions, shape decisions, and drive societal or organizational change.
- **Fosters Respect:** Respectful language demonstrates consideration for others' feelings and perspectives, promoting a harmonious environment.
- **Increases Clarity:** Clear and precise communication reduces misunderstandings and enhances efficiency in tasks and projects.
- **Shows Empathy:** Empathetic words convey compassion and support, making others feel heard and valued.
- **Leads by Example:** Using words wisely sets a standard for constructive communication, inspiring others to do the same.
- **Builds Self-Confidence:** Positive self-talk and affirming words can boost self-esteem and resilience in facing challenges.
- **Preserves Integrity:** Honest and truthful words maintain credibility and build a reputation of trustworthiness.

In social situations, people who speak less may be perceived as more respectful or wise because they listen more and speak thoughtfully. This can lead others to view them as more introspective and considerate. A clear indication of the fact that when an introvert speaks, the chances of people actually listening and taking it seriously increases. Ofcourse it has a lot to do with body language as well because if you stoop in a corner trying to avoid eye contact with anybody, it shows fear and lack of confidence in yourself.

Try to understand how you can use your words wisely in a way that benefits you, and also others around. For example, because I'm aware that people do take my advice and opinions seriously, I tend to talk about things that matter. Things that I believe would help others in some way. I write on topics that invite a new perspective to everyday things.

&

Also, talking about the importance of words, I would like to draw your attention towards the *science of affirmations.*

Affirmations are positive statements intended to influence our thoughts, behaviors, and overall mindset. At their core, affirmations are simple phrases that individuals repeat to themselves with the hope of fostering a positive mental attitude and achieving personal goals. The scientific basis for affirmations lies in understanding how our brains process and adapt to repeated thoughts.

Research supports the idea that affirmations can impact various aspects of mental health and behavior. For example, studies have shown that affirmations can reduce stress by promoting a sense of self-worth and resilience. When individuals face challenging situations, positive affirmations can help empower the mind by shifting focus away from negative self-doubt and towards more constructive self-talk.

The Importance of Affirmations in Spirituality

Affirmations are positive, powerful statements that help individuals align their thoughts, emotions, and actions with their higher goals or spiritual aspirations. In spirituality, affirmations serve as a tool to cultivate inner peace, foster self-awareness, and deepen one's connection to the divine or the universe. These simple yet transformative statements carry profound significance, helping individuals navigate the challenges of life with resilience and clarity.

One of the primary benefits of affirmations in spirituality is their ability to reprogram the mind. Our thoughts shape our reality, and affirmations are a means of consciously choosing positive and uplifting thoughts. For example, repeating phrases like "I am at peace" or "I am guided by divine wisdom" can help calm a restless mind and bring focus during meditation or prayer. By instilling positive beliefs, affirmations replace negative or limiting thought patterns that often hinder spiritual growth.

Affirmations also help individuals stay grounded in their spiritual journey. Life can be overwhelming, filled with distractions and challenges that pull people away from their inner selves. Affirmations act as anchors, reminding individuals of their spiritual values and goals. Statements like "I trust the universe" or "I am a channel for love and light" encourage faith, gratitude, and mindfulness, even in difficult times.

In addition, affirmations have the ability to foster a deeper connection with the divine. Many spiritual traditions emphasize the power of words and intentions. When spoken with sincerity and focus, affirmations can serve as prayers or mantras, opening the heart to divine guidance and love. This practice enhances one's sense of purpose and strengthens the belief that life is supported by a higher power.

By integrating affirmations into daily spiritual practices, individuals can cultivate a life of greater inner peace, self-awareness, and alignment with their highest self.

Here are some affirmations that I use in day to day life that may be of some help to the reader.

- **Affirmations for an introvert to cultivate and embrace their strengths:**

1. "I embrace my inner strength and value my unique perspective."
2. "My quiet moments are powerful; they allow me to recharge and think deeply."
3. "I trust my intuition and insights, knowing they guide me toward my true path."
4. "My solitude is a source of creativity and clarity, helping me to thrive."
5. "I am confident in my ability to make a meaningful impact through thoughtful actions."
6. "I honor my need for reflection and use it to build a resilient and grounded mindset."
7. "My quiet strength is a testament to my ability to overcome challenges with grace."
8. "I celebrate my introspective nature as a source of wisdom and personal growth."
9. "I have the power to create positive change through my unique approach and insights."
10. "I am proud of my ability to listen deeply and communicate with authenticity."
11. "My presence is valuable, and I contribute meaningfully in my own way."

12. "I find strength in my individuality and confidence in my quiet resolve."
13. "I trust that my inner world is a wellspring of strength and creativity."
14. "I am at peace with my own company and use it to cultivate inner resilience and power."
15. "I am capable of achieving my goals through focused effort and introspective wisdom."
16. "My mind is resilient, and I handle challenges with grace and strength."
17. "I am in control of my thoughts and emotions, and I choose positivity."
18. "Every day, my mental strength grows as I overcome obstacles with confidence."
19. "I embrace change and adapt effortlessly, knowing that my mind is capable and resourceful."
20. "I trust in my ability to solve problems and find solutions with clarity and creativity."
21. "My focus is sharp, and I am determined to achieve my goals with perseverance."
22. "I nurture my mind with healthy thoughts, and I am proud of my mental fortitude."
23. "I am calm under pressure, and I face life's challenges with a balanced and steady mind."
24. "I celebrate my mental achievements and continue to grow stronger each day."
25. "My mind is a powerful tool, and I use it to create positive change in my life and the lives of others."

A few more set of affirmations for overall growth:

1. "Happiness flows effortlessly into my life."
2. "I attract positive and uplifting experiences."

3. "My heart is open to happiness and love."
4. "I deserve to be happy and fulfilled."
5. "Every day, I am becoming more joyful and content."
6. "I am open to receiving abundance in all areas of my life."
7. "I am grateful for the abundance that surrounds me."
8. "I am a magnet for prosperity and positive energy."
9. "Every day, I am growing richer in all aspects of my life."
10. "Abundance is my natural state, and I embrace it fully."

The best way to use affirmations is to speak them out loud with intensity and belief.

Apart from affirmations, there is another thing one must be careful about. The words you speak everyday repeatedly without realizing may be affecting your life greatly. Do you speak about your 'problems' more often? do you use words like 'Not everything is in my hands' or constantly joke about your income being low? NOT HELPING. It is blocking the flow of abundance and happiness in your life.

Speak more words with high vibrations in day to day life such as: I love, I have, I am, etc.

XVIII

Practice Slow Mornings

Please be honest. How do you feel in the morning? Don't you miss the weekend right after waking up? and then wait for it throughout the week? You might feel that is due to laziness. But if that was the case, think of why it suddenly makes you feel energetic when you think about taking a day off?

Our bodies interpret constant hurry as a form of threat. Have you ever stopped to think about that? nature's pace is relatively slower. Everything has a certain amount of time designated to it. Therefore 'hurrying' all the time isn't natural for the human body too, which is a part of nature.

For introverts, practicing slow mornings can offer several tailored benefits that align well with their needs and preferences.

- **Here's how a slow morning routine can specifically support introverts:**

1. ***Reduced Overwhelm:*** Introverts often find social interactions and high-energy environments draining. A slow morning allows them to ease into the day at their own pace, reducing feelings of overwhelm before facing external demands.
2. ***Time for Reflection:*** Introverts typically value time for introspection. A slow morning provides uninterrupted space for reflection, journaling, or planning, which can help them feel more grounded and prepared.
3. ***Enhanced Productivity:*** By starting the day calmly and focusing on personal priorities, introverts can boost their productivity and work more effectively without the distractions or pressures of a rushed morning.
4. ***Increased Energy:*** Introverts often recharge through solitude. A slow morning routine can include activities that rejuvenate them, such as reading, meditation, or a quiet cup of coffee, helping them conserve and manage their energy levels throughout the day.
5. ***Improved Mental Health:*** Introverts might be more susceptible to feeling overwhelmed or stressed by a fast-paced start. A slow morning routine helps in maintaining mental well-being by providing a more controlled and serene environment to begin the day.
6. ***More Control Over Social Interactions:*** A calm start to the day can help introverts prepare mentally for social interactions they might face later, making these interactions less draining and more manageable.
7. ***Better Focus and Creativity:*** Introverts often excel in environments that allow for deep focus and creativity. A slow morning provides an ideal setting for engaging

in activities that stimulate their creativity and enhance concentration.

8. **Stronger Personal Boundaries:** Introverts may need more time to themselves to feel balanced. A slow morning allows them to establish personal boundaries and enjoy solitary time before engaging with others.

9. **Healthier Routines:** Introverts can use the slow morning to incorporate self-care practices that align with their needs, such as a relaxing breakfast or gentle exercise, which can contribute to overall well-being.

10. **More Effective Planning:** Introverts often prefer to plan and prepare thoughtfully. A slow morning gives them time to organize their day, set goals, and anticipate any challenges in a low-pressure setting.

ॐ

Try to wake up at least 30 mins earlier in the morning so that:

- You don't have to rush every task
- You can just sit idle for 10-15 mins and stare at your morning view outside.

If you feel like that is too much, just give it a try one day and see the difference. The slowness will bring a different level of energy and productivity within you which wouldn't have been known by you before. Where the world is trying hard to push us and make us run a race we never meant to participate in, it is a sheer pleasure keeping the mental peace alive.

There is no shame in slowness. If anything, it is the most necessary practice to inculcate in your lives in today's day and age.

Scrape time out and make it peaceful. For you. It matters more than you think.

XIX

Morning Nature Walks

Nature walks offer an environment of serenity that caters perfectly to the introverted soul. The quiet rustling of leaves, the gentle chirping of birds create a soundscape that soothes the mind and spirit. Especially for those who are spiritually inclined, nature serves as a 'tangible representation' of the divine. Observing the intricate patterns of a spider's web or the vibrant colors of a sunset reminds introverts of the interconnectedness of all things. These moments evoke a sense of wonder and humility, deepening their spiritual practice and reinforcing the belief that they are a part of something greater than themselves.

Unlike more 'social hobbies', nature walks provide an ideal balance of solitude and engagement. It's somewhat liberating. The uninterrupted time spent in nature allows for introspection, creative thinking, and mainly emotional release. Many spiritual introverts also find inspiration for journaling, art, or problem-solving during these walks, as the natural environment fosters 'clarity and imagination'. At the same time, acquaintances form in such environments way too easily. There is hardly any need for extravagant socialization or small talk. A little nod, a subtle smile, a friendly wave from afar, is all that it takes to let it be known that we are connected. We are here basking in the beauty of nature 'together'. How amazing, right?

Also, walking barefoot on grass allows us to physically connect with the Earth's electromagnetic field. This contact is more than just physical; it is a spiritual communion with the living energy of the planet. This practice is often referred to as "grounding". In many spiritual traditions, the Earth is considered a source of healing and vitality. When we walk barefoot, the soles of our feet absorb the Earth's 'negative ions', balancing our body's natural energy field. This process is said to detoxify the body, reduce inflammation, and restore equilibrium—both physically and spiritually.

The texture of the grass beneath the feet, the sensation of the soil, and the coolness of dew draw our attention to the present moment. This connection with the "now" is known to be the cornerstone of spiritual practice. In its simplicity lies profound wisdom—a call to slow down, breathe deeply, and honor the sacred bond we share with the natural world.

XX

Solo Retreats

In an increasingly connected and fast-paced world, carving out time for oneself has become a rarity rather than a norm. Solo retreats, as a hobby, provide an intentional practice of stepping back, recharging, and reconnecting with one's inner self. Whether it involves a weekend in the mountains, a day of silent meditation, or a few hours at a quiet beach, solo retreats offer transformative benefits that cater to the holistic well-being of an individual.

Solo retreats create a sacred space for allowing individuals to explore their thoughts, emotions, and goals without 'external distractions'. In solitude, people can identify 'patterns' in their behavior, clarify their aspirations, and realign their actions with their 'core values'. Such retreats often serve almost as a reset button, providing clarity and a renewed sense of purpose.

But hey! A solo retreat does not necessarily have to be boring! It can be cozy, comfortable indoors and fun!

Note: This might get a bit Nerdy :)

Let me give you a few ideas from my diary:

1. Personalized Reading Marathon

Curate a collection of books from your favorite genres or authors.

Create a cozy reading nook with blankets, pillows, and soft lighting.

Include snacks and drinks to keep the experience indulgent.

Enhance the atmosphere with ambient sounds like rain or a crackling fireplace.

2. DIY Spa Retreat

Set the mood with scented candles, essential oils, and calming music.

Enjoy activities like face masks, a warm bath with Epsom salts, or a homemade sugar scrub.

Pair the relaxation with meditation or guided visualization exercises.

3. Themed Movie Night

Pick a theme (e.g., classic comedies, fantasy adventures, or feel-good films).

Create a movie marathon playlist.

Make themed snacks or drinks to match the vibe (e.g., popcorn with creative toppings).

4. Creative Writing Retreat

Set up a dedicated space with journals, pens, and inspirational prompts.

Experiment with different forms of writing, such as poetry, short stories, or personal essays.

Consider combining the retreat with a digital detox for uninterrupted creativity.

5. Artistic Escape

Gather supplies for painting, drawing, or crafting.

Experiment with techniques like watercolor, clay modeling, or embroidery.

Let go of perfection and focus on expressing yourself through art.

6. Cooking or Baking Adventure

Choose a recipe you've never tried before and make it a culinary challenge.

Experiment with unique ingredients or cuisines.

Turn the retreat into a sensory experience by savoring each step and outcome.

7. Mindfulness and Yoga Retreat

Dedicate a day to mindfulness activities such as yoga, meditation, and breathwork.

Use online classes or apps for guidance if needed.

Incorporate moments of stillness and journaling to reflect on your experience.

8. Indoor Travel Adventure

Create an imaginary trip by immersing yourself in the culture of a place you want to visit.

Cook traditional dishes, listen to local music, and watch documentaries or movies from that region.

Learn a few basic phrases in the native language of the destination.

9. Puzzle and Game Retreat

Spend time solving jigsaw puzzles, crosswords, or Sudoku.

Dive into solo-friendly board games or online escape room games.

Challenge yourself with a strategy-based video game or card game.

10. Music and Dance Retreat

Curate a playlist of your favorite music or discover new artists.

Experiment with creating your own music using apps or instruments.

Dance like no one's watching for a mood-boosting workout.

11. Vision Board or Dream Planning

Use magazines, printouts, or art supplies to create a vision board for your dreams and goals.

Reflect on what truly matters to you and brainstorm actionable steps toward achieving your aspirations.

12. Photography Exploration

Practice photography indoors with creative lighting setups or macro photography of household objects.

Experiment with editing photos or creating a photo book of your favorite memories.

13. Gardening Indoors

Tend to indoor plants or start a small herb garden.

Experiment with plant propagation or design a mini terrarium.

Create a calming green space that doubles as a relaxation zone.

14. DIY Workshop

Work on a home improvement or DIY decor project, like painting furniture or creating wall art.

Repurpose old items into something new and functional.

Learn a new skill, like sewing or woodworking, using online tutorials.

15. Memory Lane Retreat

Revisit old photo albums, journals, or keepsakes.

Organize digital photos or create a scrapbook.

Reflect on past experiences and how they've shaped you.

Each of these ideas provides a way to enjoy solitude while engaging in activities that are both fun and fulfilling!

XXI

Meditation + Art

I do not intend to repeat cliche explanations on why meditation is important. I'm sure you know about that quite well. I'm going to therefore introduce you to something new: ***Meditation + Art.***

Art and meditation intersect in profound ways, both serving as pathways to deeper self-awareness and inner peace. Meditation cultivates a state of mindfulness and presence, allowing individuals to connect with their inner selves and explore their thoughts and emotions. Art, on the other hand, provides a medium for expressing and externalizing these inner experiences. When practiced together, art can enhance the meditative process by offering a tangible outlet for emotions and reflections that arise during meditation.

In meditation, individuals often reach a state of clarity and calm that can inspire creative expression. This creative process, through art, allows one to delve into the subconscious, revealing aspects of the self that might remain hidden. For instance, creating visual art while meditating can be a form of active contemplation, where the act of painting or sculpting becomes a meditative practice in itself.

The process of creating art—whether through drawing, painting, or sculpting—can be inherently meditative, involving a rhythmic flow and attention to detail that mirrors the mindfulness cultivated in meditation. This synergy between art and meditation ultimately enhances the individual's ability to connect with their inner world, making the experience of both practices more profound and integrated.

☙

First things first, I do not usually follow mainstream meditation techniques that might involve intentional breathing. Although I'm aware of its amazing benefits. But in order for me to continue something in the long run, I feel a need to fall in love with the process. And that happens when I do it my way. Always.

So, here are a few things I follow which you can take into account for a seemless experience:

1. I find any spiritual or mindful practice most effective immediately after a bath because of the physical as well as energetic cleansing.
2. There need not be a compulsion to sit straight, if it takes effort. Because it'll be a distraction. Sit in a position that is most comfortable to you. That's all.
3. If finding a quiet place seems challenging, put on your earplugs, and search for something on youtube called - 'Green noise' or 'brown noise' or 'rain sounds'. Download before using it to avoid ads popping up.

4. Take a Pen/Pencil and a blank paper (Or, if you prefer painting - colours). Now you're good to go.

౭౩

So how this exactly works is, you just sit calmly and amidst no distractions, focus on the 'present' and feel the void. It may feel a bit unfamiliar because in today's lifestyle there is hardly space for stillness. Your mind may take a while to actually calm down and feel the emptiness. Let time be no barrier. Take as long as you want to get in there. And once you begin to feel 'good' and 'light', open your eyes while still 'deep in the vibe' and let the pen do its magic. There are no rules, Whatever comes through, lines, patterns, words, figures just put it on the paper.

Once done, You'll be amazed by the result.

Do you recall how sometimes when you are in a deep thought, you sort of 'zone out' and start drawing random things in your diary/book?

My meditation + artwork practice has been derived from that.

Benefits:

- Your subconscious mind bleeds on the paper in front of you.
- You allow the expression of any residual emotions lying deep within.
- You may find clarity for the things about which you couldn't consciously contemplate due to lack of stillness.
- You let your nervous system calm down and feel safe in vulnerability - no one is gonna see your art.

"*Art reveals the invisible threads that connect us to the divine tapestry of existence. To create art is to channel the divine energy that flows through the cosmos, transforming it into a tangible expression of beauty.*"

XXII

Journaling: Record your Meaningful Insights

Journaling, a practice as ancient as writing itself, has evolved into a powerful tool for personal development and self-expression. This simple yet profound activity involves recording thoughts, feelings, and reflections in a written format, and it offers numerous benefits that extend beyond mere documentation. This essay explores the multifaceted nature of journaling, examining its benefits, methods, and its potential to foster personal growth.

- **The Benefits of Journaling**

Journaling serves as a versatile tool with a wide range of benefits, touching upon emotional, cognitive, and practical aspects of life.

1. ***Emotional Clarity and Regulation:*** One of the most immediate benefits of journaling is its capacity to provide emotional clarity. Writing about one's thoughts and feelings can be therapeutic, allowing individuals to process complex emotions and gain perspective. This practice can be particularly valuable during times of stress, anxiety, or emotional upheaval. By externalizing their internal experiences, individuals can achieve a sense of relief and understanding that might be difficult to attain through verbal communication alone.

2. ***Enhanced Self-Awareness:*** Journaling fosters self-awareness by encouraging individuals to reflect on their thoughts, behaviors, and experiences. Regular writing prompts introspection, helping individuals to uncover patterns in their thinking and behavior. This increased self-awareness can lead to greater insight into one's motivations, values, and goals, which is crucial for personal growth and decision-making.

3. ***Creative Expression:*** Journaling is also a powerful medium for creative expression. Whether through free writing, poetry, or creative storytelling, individuals can explore their creativity and imagination. This form of expression not only provides an outlet for artistic endeavors but also encourages problem-solving and innovation.

4. ***Goal Setting and Achievement:*** Many people use journaling as a tool for setting and tracking goals. By writing down their objectives, individuals can create a roadmap for achieving them and monitor their progress. This practice promotes accountability and motivation, as it makes goals more tangible and actionable.

ॐ

· **Methods of Journaling**

There are various methods and styles of journaling, each offering unique benefits and suited to different preferences and objectives.

1. ***Daily Journaling:*** This method involves writing regularly, often daily, to capture thoughts, events, and feelings as they occur. Daily journaling helps maintain a continuous record of experiences and can be useful for tracking personal growth over time.
2. ***Gratitude Journaling:*** Focusing on positive aspects of life, gratitude journaling involves listing things one is thankful for. This practice can enhance overall well-being by fostering a positive mindset and encouraging appreciation for the present moment.
3. ***Reflective Journaling:*** This type of journaling emphasizes self-reflection and analysis. It involves exploring specific events, decisions, or experiences to gain deeper understanding and insight. Reflective journaling is often used in personal development and therapeutic contexts.
4. ***Bullet Journaling:*** Bullet journaling combines task management with creative expression. It utilizes a structured format with bullet points, symbols, and layouts to organize tasks, goals, and ideas. This method is popular for its flexibility and adaptability to individual needs.
5. ***Stream-of-Consciousness Journaling:*** In this method, individuals write continuously without worrying about structure or grammar. This free-form approach allows for the unfiltered flow of thoughts and can uncover

subconscious insights.

☙

· **Incorporating Journaling into Daily Life**

To integrate journaling into daily life effectively, consider the following strategies:

1. ***Set Aside Time:*** Dedicate a specific time each day or week for journaling. Whether it's in the morning to set intentions or at night to reflect, consistency enhances the benefits of the practice.
2. ***Create a Comfortable Space:*** Choose a quiet and comfortable environment for journaling to encourage relaxation and focus. This space should be free from distractions and conducive to introspection.
3. ***Use Prompts:*** When starting out or experiencing writer's block, prompts can provide direction and stimulate ideas. Prompts can range from specific questions to thematic topics.
4. ***Be Honest and Authentic:*** The effectiveness of journaling relies on authenticity. Write truthfully and openly about your thoughts and feelings without concern for judgment.
5. ***Review and Reflect:*** Periodically review past entries to observe patterns and progress. This reflection can provide valuable insights and track personal development.

☙

An Introvert at heart, I thrived in solitude. I loved my evenings spent reading, snacking, or simply watching the stars from my garden. Though I was young back then and lacked the references to understand it fully, It was hard to not notice how I almost entered a 'flow state' when no one was around.

Ideas. Ideas. Ideas. Where did they come from? And for God's sake where were they in the presence of people? There seemed to be something special about my solitude! I eventually decided to write down the thoughts and epiphanies that seemed to not leave my mind at times. That is how journaling became an important part of my life. I also found that goal-setting through writing increases the likelihood of achieving personal and spiritual milestones. It allowed me to reflect on my growth over time, celebrating successes and learning from setbacks, along with fostering resilience and spiritual maturity.

For spiritually inclined individuals, journaling can be a profound practice that fosters a deeper connection with their inner selves and the divine. Research published in the Journal of Psychology and Theology has shown that mindfulness practices, including reflective journaling, are associated with greater spiritual well-being.

In many spiritual traditions, journaling serves as a form of prayer or meditation. Writing down prayers, affirmations, or gratitude entries allows individuals to communicate with the divine in a personal and meaningful way. Research from Harvard University has found that practices like gratitude journaling can improve emotional resilience and increase feelings of interconnectedness, both of which are essential components of spiritual growth. Journaling, in this context, becomes more than a habit—it becomes a sacred ritual.

Spirituality is often synonymous with transformation—a journey of becoming one's best self. Journaling supports this by serving as a 'record of progress' and a tool for setting intentions for the future making it a cornerstone of modern spiritual practice.

"

Introverts possess a unique creative power: the ability to turn quiet moments into masterpieces and introspective thoughts into brilliant ideas."

XXIII

Declutter your Space

The environment we live in or spend most of the time in, has proven impacts on our mind and body. Being an introvert and therefore sensitive to energy, try to be mindful of the things you surround yourself with. Any unnecessary clutter may contain stuck energy and create confusion in the mind without realizing! It also sometimes has the potential to encourage procrastinating behaviour. Which is quite common these days.

Decluttering positively affects the mind through several scientific mechanisms. Excessive clutter can overwhelm the brain, making it difficult to concentrate and process information. This phenomenon is linked to cognitive overload, where the brain's resources are stretched thin, reducing efficiency. Research shows that a clutter-free environment can lower cortisol levels, a stress hormone, thereby reducing anxiety and promoting relaxation. Additionally, organizing one's space can trigger a sense of accomplishment and control, which boosts overall mental well-being and satisfaction. This enhanced mental state allows for improved focus and productivity, creating a cycle of positive reinforcement in cognitive and emotional health.

Each time you look at a huge pile of things that need to be sorted and arranged, even the thought of spending hours into dealing with it may feel tiring. But it is scientifically proven that cleaning/decluttering your space may take some time but once done, creates a sense of achievement and enables the release of 'dopamine'- the feel good hormone.

But remember to not 'force' anything because it may not last. Instead, create a plan.

Even I did not know that there theories exist! have a look:

ॐ

- **There are several effective methods for decluttering your surroundings, each catering to different needs and preferences. Here are some popular approaches:**

1. ***The KonMari Method:*** Developed by Marie Kondo, this method involves decluttering by category rather than location. You start with clothing, then move on to books, papers, komono (miscellaneous items), and finally sentimental items. The key principle is to keep only those items that "spark joy."

2. ***The 20/20 Rule:*** This method, popularized by YouTuber Matt D'Avella, suggests that if an item can be replaced for under $20 and in under 20 minutes, it should be discarded rather than kept. This rule helps in making

quick decisions about whether to keep or toss items.

3. ***The Four-Box Method:*** This approach involves labeling four boxes as "Keep," "Donate," "Sell," and "Trash." Items are sorted into these boxes to streamline the decluttering process, making it easier to decide the fate of each item.

4. ***The Minimalist Approach:*** This method focuses on adopting a minimalist lifestyle by reducing possessions to only those that are essential or bring significant value. It often involves a broader lifestyle change, aiming for simplicity and intentionality in one's possessions.

5. ***The One-In, One-Out Rule:*** To maintain a clutter-free environment, this rule states that for every new item brought into the home, an existing item should be removed. This helps in controlling the accumulation of belongings over time.

6. ***The 30-Day Minimalism Challenge:*** This method involves removing a set number of items each day for 30 days. It starts with one item on the first day, two on the second day, and so on, gradually increasing the number of items removed. This approach encourages consistent decluttering and can be less overwhelming.

7. ***The Room-by-Room Approach:*** This method involves tackling one room or area at a time, which can make the task of decluttering more manageable. It allows for focused effort and ensures that each space is thoroughly organized.

8. ***The Time-Based Approach:*** Setting a specific amount of time, such as 15 or 30 minutes, for decluttering each day helps in making the process less daunting. This approach encourages regular, manageable sessions of decluttering.

9. ***The Digital Declutter:*** Involves organizing and reducing digital clutter, such as emails, files, and apps. This method helps in improving digital productivity and reducing mental overload from a cluttered digital workspace.

10. ***The "Minimalist Game":*** Popularized by The Minimalists, this game involves removing a number of items equal to the day of the month. For example, on the first day, you remove one item; on the second day, two items, and so forth. It turns decluttering into a fun and progressive challenge.

❧

Each method offers a unique approach to decluttering, allowing individuals to choose one that best fits their needs, preferences, and lifestyle.

❧

There is a secret technique I would like to share for my lazy friends out there :)

On the days you feel too lazy, try arranging everything in either horizontal or vertical lines. You will not even feel any effort and yet everything will look pretty clean. I used to follow this thing for a very long time until I realized after some research that it infact has some scientific backing.

The "lazy" way of decluttering your space, often referred to as the method of arranging everything both horizontally and vertically, focuses on simplifying organization with minimal effort. This approach leverages spatial efficiency and visual clarity to create a less cluttered environment. Here's how you can implement it:

- **Horizontal Arranging**

1. ***Surface Organization:*** Start by clearing off flat surfaces like countertops, desks, and tables. Group similar items together and use trays or containers to keep things organized. This helps in reducing visual clutter and makes it easier to find what you need.
2. ***Use of Shelving:*** Install shelves at various heights to utilize wall space effectively. Place frequently used items within easy reach and less frequently used items higher up. This prevents surfaces from becoming cluttered while maintaining accessibility.

- **Vertical Arranging**

1. ***Stacking Items:*** Arrange items vertically by stacking them in neat piles. For example, books can be stacked horizontally, and storage boxes can be stacked vertically. This method maximizes space and keeps items visible and accessible.
2. ***Vertical Storage Solutions:*** Use vertical storage solutions like tall bookcases, cabinets with multiple shelves, or hanging organizers. This approach frees up floor space and keeps items organized within a compact footprint.

- **Dual Orientation**

1. ***Combine Horizontal and Vertical Storage:*** For example, use drawer dividers to organize items within a drawer (horizontal organization) while stacking smaller containers or boxes within the drawer for added vertical storage. This combination helps in maintaining order and optimizing space.

2. *Labeling:* Use labels on containers or shelves to indicate the contents. This minimizes the time spent searching for items and encourages consistent organization.

- **Declutter in Phases**

1. *Incremental Sorting:* Tackle one category or area at a time, arranging items both horizontally and vertically as you go. This prevents overwhelm and makes the process more manageable.
2. *Regular Maintenance:* Schedule periodic reviews to maintain organization. Reassess and adjust arrangements to ensure items remain easily accessible and the space stays clutter-free.

This method's "lazy" appeal lies in its simplicity and ease of implementation. By focusing on arranging items horizontally and vertically, you can effectively reduce clutter without extensive effort. It's a practical approach for those looking for a straightforward way to achieve a more organized and visually appealing space.

the more your surroundings are organized, the more clarity there is in your overall aura. Yes. Again the interconnectedness of the universal energies :)

XXIV

Routine and Flexibility

If you look around, almost every other life coach asks you to follow a 'daily routine' to live your life to its fullest potential. In our fast-paced world, where each day brings new challenges and opportunities, the importance of routine in life cannot be overstated. A routine provides structure and organization, making our lives more manageable and productive. It serves as a framework that allows us to prioritize tasks, set goals, and achieve them efficiently. And I totally agree with that. It makes a lot of sense.

A Few key advantages of routine are:

· *Having a routine helps us establish good habits.*

When we follow a consistent schedule, whether it's waking up at the same time each day, exercising regularly, or setting aside specific hours for work or study, these actions become ingrained in our daily lives.

· *Routine also reduces stress and anxiety by eliminating 'uncertainty'.*

When we know what to expect and have a plan in place, we feel more in control of our circumstances. This sense of control boosts our confidence and allows us to approach challenges with a clearer mind.

· *Routine fosters self-discipline.*

By committing to a schedule, we learn the importance of consistency and perseverance. This discipline extends beyond our daily tasks; it influences our ability to stay focused on long-term goals and pursue them with dedication.

· *Routine also plays an important role in improving time management skills.*

When we allocate specific time slots for different activities, we become more efficient in how we use our time. This efficiency translates into increased productivity and the ability to accomplish more in less time.

· ***Routines promote better health and well-being.***

Regular exercise, balanced meals, and sufficient sleep are essential components of a healthy routine.

When these activities become part of our daily schedule, they contribute to our physical and mental resilience, improving overall quality of life.

But what looks good in theory often becomes a little difficult to follow through in the long term. I'm sure many people will relate with starting something with a lot of gist and then eventually giving up without even realizing. Excuses may be infinite, but it boils down to one reason - Rigidity.

Our daily lives have been programmed into structures forcefully such as having to sleep and wake up at a certain time due to work, or having to eat at a certain time because well.. That's lunch time at work. The food you eat most of the time depends on what you can arrange in a limited time in the morning. Not what you really 'want'. The clothes you wear depend on what is allowed at work, not necessarily what you 'love'. Due to this, whatever little time or bandwidth remains in our lives, it subconsciously demands 'freedom'.

There is a very interesting concept about sleep patterns in modern human beings known as *'revenge bedtime procrastination'.* Its widespread recognition and understanding stem from collective observations and discussions among psychologists, sleep researchers.

Revenge bedtime procrastination typically describes the behavior where individuals without realizing, deliberately stay awake later than necessary at night, often sacrificing sleep, as a way to 'reclaim' personal time and leisure after a day filled with responsibilities, work, or obligations. It's seen as a form of subconscious rebellion against the feeling of not having enough control or free time during the day.

I used to watch my father stay up till midnight for no reason. I often wondered why? Why couldn't he just sleep early when he had to leave for work the next morning? And I understand that now. Without a doubt I do. After watching all my amazing habits getting crushed to the ground, I began to see the patterns of why. So I decided that we deserved the limited amount of flexibility that was available. But the real magic happened when I questioned - why can't routines be flexible? Without overwhelming the mind with yet another set of rigid structure? And that is how I recollected the pieces of my lost passion - Mindful living & Self love.

I created a routine that is highly flexible and yet, set to a certain pattern that is healthy.

For example, I drink Matcha tea almost every morning. But sometimes I switch it up with different drinks like amla (Indian gooseberry) juice, jaggery-sweetened lassi (cold yogurt drink) or even monk-fruit-sweetened dark chocolate shake. No matter what I drink, the pattern remains - I drink something healthy in the morning.

No routine will ever do good to you if it feels like yet another 'task'.

You should have discovered by now the importance of the 'feel good factor' in almost every area of human life to truly prosper. Pain is not the necessary answer for everything. Especially if you are a sensitive introvert. Don't punish yourself. A routine should feel 'effortless and interesting'. Only then will it stay longer and do 'actual' good. I would love to see you cut a slack from the life that forces rigidity and through 'flexible routine', eventually reclaim your physical and mental well being. Live your life to the fullest. Because you deserve it. Of all the people out there, YOU were not born to be a machine.

XXV

Exercise for Introverts

Exercise is beneficial to everyone who has a body irrespective of gender, age or socializing preferences.

Incorporating exercise into your routine can have profound and wide-ranging benefits, affecting nearly every aspect of your health and well-being.

But why is it particularly beneficial for introverts?

- **The Physical Aspect:**

Achieving and maintaining a good physique often boosts self-esteem and confidence, which can positively affect various aspects of life, including personal and professional interactions. Being subconciously aware of the fact that you 'do' have a good physique which most people want but don't have the drive to cultivate, adds an X factor to your self-image.

Even if no one came at you with praises the moment you enter a room, lets be honest the intrigue is quite visible. You can see it in the way people subtly exchange glances and look at you thinking you aren't aware.

Most introverts can relate to feeling lesser often due to the inability to be loud which honestly is quite sad and common. Now. Imagine your outer demeanor speaking volumes about who you are without you, having to make any 'conscious' effort.

Ofcourse no one should be judged based on what they look like, but don't you think it happens all the time even without a thought?

While physical appearance is not the only measure of worth, societal norms often associate a good physique with health and vitality, which can positively influence how others perceive and interact with you.

When you look at someone with a good physique, it automatically tells you a lot about that person:

1) They're disciplined. It takes consistency to shed those extra pounds or gain those abs.

2) They're Hardworking. It takes a lot to go past all pain and lethargy to show up everyday in order to truly see a difference.

3) They have 'high self worth.' Why do I say that? Because it surprisingly takes a lot to make most people watch what they eat and drink even after so many health and wellness influencers have successfully made it 'trendy'.

The most important thing remains - when you look at yourself in the mirror and love what you see, your confidence skyrockets. And without a word, it SHOWS. And puts people in awe of you.

❧

- **The Mental Aspect:**

Physical fitness is closely linked to mental well-being. Regular exercise and a healthy physique can reduce symptoms of depression, anxiety, and stress, contributing to a more positive outlook on life.

Exercise stimulates the release of endorphins, often referred to as "feel-good" hormones. These chemicals interact with the brain's receptors to reduce 'pain perception' and create a sense of euphoria, commonly known as the 'runner's high.'3

Exercise affects neurotransmitters like serotonin, dopamine, and norepinephrine, which are crucial for mood regulation.

Physical activity enhances cognitive functions such as attention, memory, and executive function. Regular exercise has been shown to increase the size of the hippocampus, a brain area involved in memory and learning.

Negative effects of the stress hormone 'cortisol' is no more a secret due to an entire generation experiencing various health issue that weren't so common until few years back. Exercise lowers levels of cortisol. This reduction in cortisol, along with the endorphin release, helps alleviate stress and promotes a more relaxed state of mind.

And a relaxed state of mind becomes potent in clarity of thoughts and opinions

Another interesting mental aspect of exercise is that physical hard work can enhance mental resilience by promoting focus, and persistence. Overcoming physical challenges can translate into 'increased psychological toughness' and a greater ability to handle whatever life throws at you.

༄

- **Emotional Aspect:**

Talking about introverts and not discussing emotions?

Exercise often involves social elements, these interactions can improve social skills and provide 'emotional support', further benefiting the emotional health of an introvert.

For those introverts who want to engage in social settings, but not with a lot of extravagance, exercise can offer structured environments, like fitness classes or sports teams, where interactions are based around a shared activity rather than open-ended socializing.

This creates a sense of security as the point of any conversation revolves mostly around the particular exercise or activity they are involved in.

Since most people in either sports or exercise carry a 'growth + supportive' mindset, it can add as an amazing motivating factor in an introvert's life.

When I went to the gym for the first time, it was surprisingly easier for me to talk to anyone around because each and every person there was working hard and understood the importance of support and a collaborative environment.

When I began exercising without a personal trainer, I had people walk up to me and provide guidance without even asking. But why? I believe that is because they have been through the grind and know what it feels like to be a beginer.

And the emotional satisfaction in seeing people support and hype each other, is off the charts for me.

In conclusion, I urge you to try commiting to whatever exercise best suits you - gym, yoga, zumba, running, cycling etc.

You will definitely experience upliftment physically, mentally as well as emotionally.

Part 3

XXVI

The Quiet Genius—Albert Einstein's Introverted Brilliance

In a world often enamored with the dazzling spectacle of 'extroverted achievement', Albert Einstein stands as a testament to the profound power of introversion. His journey from a quiet, introspective youth to one of history's greatest minds offers a compelling narrative of how introverted traits can lead to monumental contributions to humanity.

The Solitude of Thought

Albert Einstein was not just a theoretical physicist; he was a thinker who thrived in solitude. Born in Ulm, Germany, in 1879, Einstein's early years were marked by a deep engagement with his inner world. His inclination toward introspection and solitary study set him apart from his peers. As a child, he would spend hours lost in thought, exploring complex ideas that others might find daunting.

Einstein's introversion was not simply a personality trait but a source of his intellectual strength. While his extroverted counterparts engaged in lively debates and social interactions, Einstein found his insights in quiet reflection and solitary contemplation. It was in these moments of solitude that he unraveled the mysteries of the universe, formulating theories that would forever alter the landscape of physics.

The Power of Solitary Reflection

Einstein's preference for solitude was evident throughout his life. In his early career, while working at the Swiss Patent Office, Einstein's job involved evaluating patents for inventions. While this might seem a mundane task, it provided him with ample time for introspection. It was during these quiet hours, away from the academic hustle and bustle, that Einstein developed his groundbreaking theories of special relativity.

The very nature of his work demanded an environment free from the distractions of constant social engagement. Einstein's ability to immerse himself in deep, solitary thought allowed him to develop revolutionary ideas that challenged the very fabric of classical physics. His famous equation, $E=mc^2$, was born from this profound, introspective process, reshaping our understanding of energy and matter.

The Introverted Scholar

Einstein's introversion was not just about preference but also about method. His approach to problem-solving was deeply reflective. Rather than seeking immediate validation from peers, he would retreat into his own mind, exploring the ramifications of his theories in a self-contained environment. This introspective method enabled him to think deeply and creatively, leading to breakthroughs that were initially met with skepticism but later celebrated as foundational principles in physics.

His lectures and public appearances, though less frequent, were marked by a deep, contemplative presence. Einstein's public speaking was characterized by a quiet confidence and a profound sense of purpose. He would often address audiences not with flamboyance but with a calm, measured delivery that reflected his inner certainty and intellectual depth.

Challenges and Triumphs

Einstein's introverted nature also meant he faced challenges in a world that often valued extroverted qualities. His unconventional ideas initially met with resistance from the scientific community. The general theory of relativity, for instance, was a radical departure from classical physics and took years to gain acceptance.

Yet, it was his introverted qualities—his resilience, patience, and unwavering commitment to his ideas—that allowed him to persevere. His quiet determination and deep engagement with his theories eventually led to validation through empirical evidence, such as the famous observation of the bending of starlight during a solar eclipse, which confirmed his predictions and cemented his place in scientific history.

Legacy of Quiet Influence

Einstein's legacy extends beyond his scientific achievements. His life demonstrates how introversion can be a powerful force for innovation and insight. His ability to work alone, think deeply, and remain steadfast in the face of adversity has inspired countless individuals to embrace their own introverted strengths.

In a world that often celebrates loud and flashy accomplishments, Einstein's story serves as a reminder of the profound impact that quiet introspection and solitary dedication can have. His life and work challenge us to recognize the value of introverted qualities and to appreciate the silent yet powerful contributions they can make to the world.

Conclusion

Albert Einstein's introverted nature was not a mere backdrop to his genius but a crucial component of it. His ability to delve deeply into his thoughts, to find solace and inspiration in solitude, and to challenge established norms with quiet resolve illustrates the remarkable power of introversion. As we reflect on his extraordinary contributions, we are reminded that greatness can emerge from the quiet corners of our minds, and that the introverted path, while less conspicuous, is no less potent in shaping the world.

XXVII

Marie Curie - The Quiet Innovator

In the realm of scientific achievement, Marie Curie shines as a beacon of quiet brilliance and resilience. Her extraordinary contributions to science—most notably her groundbreaking work on radioactivity—reveal how an introverted nature can lead to profound discoveries and lasting impact. Curie's life and work exemplify the transformative power of introspection, solitude, and focused dedication.

The Solitude of Discovery

Marie Curie, born Maria Skłodowska in 1867 in Warsaw, Poland, was a woman whose genius flourished in the solitude of her scientific endeavors. From a young age, Curie exhibited a profound dedication to her studies, often finding solace in the pursuit of knowledge. Her introverted nature allowed her to immerse herself deeply in the world of science, away from the distractions of social conventions and public acclaim.

Curie's path to scientific excellence was not a crowded one but rather a solitary journey of intellectual discovery. Her move to Paris to study at the Sorbonne marked a pivotal moment in her life. There, she worked in a small, makeshift laboratory with her husband, Pierre Curie. The conditions were modest, the resources limited, but it was in this quiet space of focused effort that Curie made some of her most significant discoveries.

The Quiet Strength of Focused Work

Curie's introversion was reflected in her approach to scientific research. She was known for her methodical and solitary work habits, often spending long hours in the laboratory. Her dedication to her research on radioactivity required intense focus and perseverance. Unlike many of her contemporaries who thrived in collaborative and social settings, Curie found her greatest strength in the quiet and contemplative aspects of her work.

Her work on the discovery of radium and polonium—elements that were previously unknown to science—was achieved through rigorous experimentation and analysis. Curie's ability to work alone and her deep concentration allowed her to conduct meticulous research, leading to discoveries that would revolutionize the field of physics and chemistry.

Challenges and Triumphs

Despite her introverted disposition, Curie faced numerous challenges. As a woman in a male-dominated field, she encountered significant barriers and skepticism. Her dedication to her work was often accompanied by personal and professional hurdles, including the loss of her husband Pierre to a tragic accident. Yet, it was her introverted qualities—her resilience, inner strength, and unwavering commitment to science—that helped her overcome these obstacles.

Curie's solitary perseverance led to monumental achievements. She was awarded the Nobel Prize in Physics in 1903, alongside Pierre Curie and Henri Becquerel, for their work on radioactivity. Her subsequent Nobel Prize in Chemistry in 1911, awarded for her discoveries of radium and polonium, further solidified her status as one of the greatest scientists of her time. Curie's ability to remain focused and dedicated in the face of adversity highlights the power of introverted qualities in achieving greatness.

Legacy of Quiet Influence

Marie Curie's legacy extends far beyond her scientific discoveries. Her life story serves as a powerful testament to the impact of introverted traits on the world stage. Curie's introspection, patience, and solitary dedication were instrumental in her achievements. Her work not only advanced scientific knowledge but also paved the way for future generations of scientists, particularly women, in a field that was once considered inaccessible.

Curie's contributions to science also had practical implications, including advancements in medical treatments and diagnostics through radiation therapy. Her discoveries have had a profound impact on medicine and technology, showcasing how the quiet work of an introverted individual can lead to advancements that benefit humanity.

Conclusion

Marie Curie's introverted nature was not a hindrance but a cornerstone of her extraordinary achievements. Her ability to work independently, her focused dedication, and her resilience in the face of challenges reveal the remarkable power of introversion in scientific innovation. As we reflect on her legacy, we are reminded that greatness can emerge from the quiet spaces of our minds, and that the introverted path, while often solitary, can lead to transformative contributions that shape the world. Curie's life and work inspire us to recognize and celebrate the profound impact that introverted qualities can have on our collective progress and well-being.

XXVIII

J.K. Rowling-The Quiet Magician of Imagination

In a world that often celebrates loud and public achievements, J.K. Rowling's story stands as a powerful testament to the quiet strength of introversion. The author of the globally beloved "Harry Potter" series transformed the landscape of modern literature through her introverted nature—a journey that underscores how solitude and introspection can foster extraordinary creativity and resilience.

The Solitude of Storytelling

Joanne Rowling, known to the world as J.K. Rowling, began her journey in relative obscurity, with a quiet resolve that was as unassuming as it was profound. Born in Yate, Gloucestershire, in 1965, Rowling's early years were marked by a deep love for reading and storytelling. Her introverted nature, characterized by a preference for solitude and deep reflection, was instrumental in shaping her creative process.

Rowling's path to literary success was not immediate. After graduating from the University of Exeter, she faced a series of personal and professional setbacks, including the death of her mother and a period of economic hardship. During this challenging time, Rowling found solace in the creation of her magical world. Her introversion allowed her to retreat into her imagination, crafting the intricate and immersive universe of Hogwarts while navigating the struggles of everyday life.

The Power of Introverted Creativity

Rowling's introverted traits—her introspective nature, focus, and love for solitary work—played a crucial role in the development of the "Harry Potter" series. Writing the first book, "Harry Potter and the Philosopher's Stone" (known as "Harry Potter and the Sorcerer's Stone" in the U.S.), was a deeply personal endeavor. Rowling often worked in quiet coffee shops, finding inspiration and escape from the challenges she faced. Her solitary writing sessions allowed her to delve deeply into the characters and the magical world she was creating.

The depth and detail of the "Harry Potter" series are a testament to Rowling's introverted creativity. Her ability to spend long hours in isolation, crafting complex plots and vivid characters, resulted in a series that captivated millions of readers worldwide. The success of the books reflects the power of introverted qualities in fostering creativity that resonates deeply with others.

Challenges and Triumphs

Rowling's journey to success was fraught with challenges, including rejection from multiple publishers and personal struggles as a single mother. Her introverted nature was tested as she navigated these obstacles. Yet, it was her quiet determination and resilience that ultimately led to her breakthrough. The perseverance of her introverted spirit allowed her to continue refining her work, despite the setbacks.

When "Harry Potter and the Philosopher's Stone" was finally published, it marked the beginning of a phenomenon that would redefine children's literature. The series not only achieved commercial success but also garnered critical acclaim, touching the lives of readers of all ages. Rowling's introverted qualities, such as her ability to deeply reflect on her characters and themes, contributed to the rich, emotional depth of the series.

Legacy of Quiet Inspiration

J.K. Rowling's story is more than just a tale of literary success; it is a reflection of how introverted traits can lead to profound and lasting impact. Her journey from struggling single mother to global literary icon demonstrates that introversion can be a powerful force in achieving greatness. Rowling's ability to channel her introspection and solitude into the creation of a beloved literary universe has inspired countless individuals.

Beyond her literary achievements, Rowling's philanthropic efforts and advocacy work have further solidified her legacy. Her quiet dedication to causes such as children's rights and poverty alleviation showcases how introverted strengths can extend beyond personal success to make a meaningful difference in the world.

Conclusion

J.K. Rowling's introverted nature was not a limitation but a wellspring of creative and personal strength. Her ability to work alone, to find inspiration in solitude, and to persevere through challenges exemplifies the remarkable power of introversion. As we reflect on her achievements, we are reminded that greatness often emerges from the quiet spaces of our minds, and that the introverted path, while often solitary, can lead to extraordinary accomplishments that touch the lives of millions. Rowling's life and work inspire us to embrace and celebrate the profound impact of introverted qualities, showing that true magic lies in the quiet power of the imagination.

XXIX

Bill Gates - The Quiet Visionary Behind the Screen

In the world of technology and philanthropy, Bill Gates stands out not only for his immense achievements but also for the quiet, introspective nature that has underpinned his success. As the co-founder of Microsoft and a leading philanthropist, Gates's introverted qualities have played a pivotal role in shaping his career and driving his impact on the world. His story exemplifies how introversion can be a powerful catalyst for innovation and meaningful change.

The Solitude of Innovation

Born in Seattle in 1955, Bill Gates exhibited a keen interest in computers from an early age. His journey into the world of technology began in solitude, driven by an intense curiosity and a desire to understand the emerging field of computing. Gates's introverted nature allowed him to delve deeply into programming and software development, often spending long hours in isolation honing his skills and exploring new ideas.

Gates's early experiences with computers were characterized by a solitary pursuit of knowledge. While his peers engaged in typical teenage activities, Gates immersed himself in the intricate world of coding and systems design. His ability to focus intensely and work alone was crucial in the development of Microsoft's first software products, setting the stage for the company's future success.

The Power of Quiet Determination

Gates's introverted qualities are evident in his approach to problem-solving and innovation. Unlike many of his contemporaries who thrived on public appearances and high-profile networking, Gates preferred a more subdued approach. His focus was on the technology itself and the potential it held for transforming the world. His quiet determination and analytical mindset allowed him to tackle complex problems and envision solutions that others might overlook.

The creation of the MS-DOS operating system and the subsequent development of the Windows operating system are testaments to Gates's introverted work ethic. His ability to concentrate on the technical aspects of software and to refine and improve upon existing technologies was instrumental in Microsoft's rise to prominence. Gates's behind-the-scenes efforts and meticulous attention to detail laid the foundation for one of the most influential technology companies in history.

Challenges and Strategic Vision

Throughout his career, Gates faced numerous challenges, from fierce competition to technological hurdles. His introverted nature, characterized by a preference for deep thinking and strategic planning, enabled him to navigate these challenges with a level-headed approach. Gates's ability to remain focused and resilient, despite external pressures, played a critical role in Microsoft's growth and adaptation in the rapidly evolving tech industry.

Gates's transition from CEO of Microsoft to a full-time philanthropist also highlights his introverted strengths. The Bill & Melinda Gates Foundation, established in 2000, reflects Gates's quiet commitment to addressing global issues such as health, education, and poverty. His approach to philanthropy is marked by a data-driven, thoughtful strategy, emphasizing research, evidence-based solutions, and long-term impact.

Legacy of Quiet Impact

Bill Gates's introverted nature has significantly influenced his legacy. His work in technology revolutionized personal computing and software development, impacting millions of lives around the world. His philanthropic efforts have addressed pressing global challenges, improving health outcomes, and advancing educational opportunities.

Gates's story illustrates how introversion can be a powerful force for innovation and social good. His ability to work independently, think strategically, and approach problems with a calm, methodical mindset has allowed him to achieve remarkable success and make a profound difference in the world.

Conclusion

Bill Gates's journey from a quiet, introspective young programmer to a global technology leader and philanthropist demonstrates the profound impact of introverted traits. His ability to focus intensely, work behind the scenes, and approach challenges with a thoughtful, strategic mindset has shaped his career and his contributions to society. As we reflect on Gates's achievements, we are reminded that introversion is not a barrier to success but a source of strength and innovation. Gates's life and work inspire us to embrace the quiet power of introversion, showing that even in a world that often celebrates extroverted qualities, the greatest accomplishments can emerge from the solitude of introspective thought and strategic vision.

XXX

Stephen Hawking - The Quiet Luminary of the Cosmos

In the realm of scientific achievement and intellectual brilliance, Stephen Hawking's story is a profound testament to the power of introversion. As a theoretical physicist and cosmologist, Hawking's remarkable contributions to our understanding of the universe were profoundly shaped by his introverted nature. His journey from a young student with a keen intellect to a globally renowned scientist demonstrates how solitude, introspection, and resilience can lead to groundbreaking discoveries and enduring influence.

The Solitude of Cosmic Exploration

Stephen Hawking was born in Oxford, England, in 1942, during a time of great global turmoil. From an early age, he exhibited a fascination with the cosmos and the nature of existence. His introverted nature allowed him to immerse himself deeply in the mysteries of theoretical physics and cosmology. Hawking's preference for solitary reflection and deep thought was evident throughout his academic career, enabling him to explore complex concepts that would later redefine our understanding of the universe.

Hawking's academic journey was marked by long hours of solitary study and contemplation. As a student at University College Oxford and later at Cambridge, he devoted himself to unraveling the fundamental principles of cosmology and black hole physics. His introverted inclination to think independently and explore ideas in isolation provided him with the focus needed to tackle some of the most challenging questions in science.

The Power of Quiet Intellect

Hawking's introversion was a crucial element in his approach to scientific inquiry. His ability to work independently, to delve deeply into complex theories, and to remain focused on his research was central to his success. His seminal work on black holes and the nature of the universe was characterized by a meticulous, introspective approach to problem-solving.

One of Hawking's most profound contributions was his theory of black hole evaporation, which emerged from his deep contemplation of the nature of black holes and quantum mechanics. His introduction of the concept of Hawking radiation challenged existing theories and provided new insights into the behavior of black holes, fundamentally altering our understanding of the cosmos. This breakthrough was a direct result of his ability to think deeply and work quietly on complex problems.

Challenges and Quiet Courage

Stephen Hawking's life was marked by significant personal and professional challenges. Diagnosed with amyotrophic lateral sclerosis (ALS) at the age of 21, Hawking faced a debilitating illness that gradually impaired his physical abilities. Despite these challenges, his introverted nature allowed him to persevere and continue his work with extraordinary determination.

Hawking's resilience in the face of adversity was reflected in his ability to communicate complex scientific ideas to a broad audience, despite his physical limitations. His use of a speech-generating device and his ability to convey profound concepts through writing and public speaking highlighted his courage and unwavering commitment to his work. His introverted strength—his focus, intellectual curiosity, and determination—enabled him to make significant contributions to science even as he navigated the challenges of his condition.

Legacy of Introverted Brilliance

Stephen Hawking's legacy is a testament to the profound impact of introverted qualities. His contributions to theoretical physics and cosmology have had a lasting influence on our understanding of the universe. Hawking's ability to work independently, to engage deeply with complex theories, and to persist through personal challenges exemplifies the power of introversion in achieving extraordinary accomplishments.

Beyond his scientific achievements, Hawking's efforts to popularize science and inspire curiosity about the universe reflect the broader impact of his introverted nature. His books, such as "A Brief History of Time," made complex scientific concepts accessible to millions and encouraged a new generation to explore the wonders of the cosmos. His legacy extends to his role as a mentor and advocate for scientific exploration, demonstrating how introverted strengths can contribute to public understanding and appreciation of science.

Conclusion

Stephen Hawking's story is a powerful reminder of the extraordinary achievements that can arise from introversion. His ability to focus deeply, to work independently, and to persevere through personal and professional challenges allowed him to make profound contributions to our understanding of the universe. As we reflect on Hawking's life and work, we are reminded that introverted qualities can be a source of immense strength and inspiration. His journey from a young thinker to a global luminary demonstrates that the quiet power of introspection and intellectual dedication can lead to groundbreaking discoveries and a lasting impact on the world.

XXXI

Swami Vivekananda - The Quiet Catalyst of Global Spiritual Awakening

In the rich tapestry of Indian spirituality, Swami Vivekananda stands out as a figure of profound influence and enduring legacy. His remarkable journey from a contemplative young seeker to a globally recognized spiritual leader illustrates how introversion can serve as a powerful catalyst for spiritual awakening and global change. Vivekananda's introverted nature, marked by deep introspection and inner dedication, played a crucial role in shaping his teachings and his impact on the world.

The Solitude of Spiritual Quest

Swami Vivekananda, born Narendranath Datta in 1863, grew up in a world of bustling cultural and political change. From a young age, Vivekananda exhibited a deep intellectual curiosity and a tendency towards introspection. His early experiences with spirituality were characterized by long hours of solitary meditation and study. This introverted nature allowed him to delve deeply into the philosophies of Vedanta and Yoga, setting the stage for his future spiritual leadership.

Vivekananda's time spent in solitary contemplation under the guidance of his master, Sri Ramakrishna, was a period of profound inner exploration. It was in the quietude of his own mind that Vivekananda grappled with existential questions and sought answers about the nature of reality and the self. His introverted approach to spiritual practice was not an escape from the world but a method for penetrating its deeper truths.

The Power of Quiet Reflection

Vivekananda's introversion was instrumental in the development of his spiritual teachings. His ability to reflect deeply and to internalize complex spiritual concepts allowed him to articulate profound insights with clarity and conviction. His teachings on the universality of religions, the divinity within every individual, and the importance of self-realization were deeply rooted in his own introspective experiences.

One of Vivekananda's most influential contributions was his address at the Parliament of the World's Religions in Chicago in 1893. Despite his initial shyness and the significant public speaking challenge, Vivekananda's profound reflections on the unity of all religions and the spiritual potential of humanity resonated with audiences around the world. His introverted strength—his deep inner understanding and his contemplative insights—allowed him to speak with a rare authenticity that captivated and inspired listeners.

Challenges and Quiet Determination

Vivekananda's path was not without its challenges. He faced numerous obstacles, including financial difficulties and personal doubts. His introverted nature often meant that he preferred solitude and reflection over social engagement, which sometimes led to misunderstandings and isolation. Yet, it was precisely this introverted resolve that allowed him to remain focused on his mission despite external difficulties.

Vivekananda's quiet determination and resilience were evident in his tireless efforts to promote the teachings of Vedanta and to establish the Ramakrishna Mission. His introverted strength helped him to persevere through periods of hardship and to continue his work of spreading spiritual knowledge both in India and abroad.

Legacy of Quiet Inspiration

Swami Vivekananda's legacy is a testament to the profound impact of introverted qualities on global spiritual consciousness. His ability to translate deep spiritual insights into practical teachings and his emphasis on self-realization and universal brotherhood continue to inspire millions. His work in establishing the Ramakrishna Mission has left an indelible mark on social service and spiritual education.

Vivekananda's writings and speeches, including his influential book "Raja Yoga," offer a blend of philosophical depth and practical wisdom that reflects his introverted approach to spirituality. His emphasis on meditation, self-discipline, and the inner life underscores how introversion can be a source of profound strength and insight.

Conclusion

Swami Vivekananda's life and teachings highlight the transformative power of introversion in the realm of spirituality. His journey from a solitary seeker to a global spiritual leader demonstrates that deep introspection and quiet reflection can lead to extraordinary contributions and a lasting impact on the world. Vivekananda's ability to harness his introverted nature for the pursuit of spiritual truth and to share his insights with a global audience serves as a powerful reminder that the quiet path of inner exploration can lead to profound awakening and inspiration. His legacy invites us to embrace the strengths of introversion, showing that even in the midst of global influence and public engagement, the true power of spirituality often emerges from the quiet depths of the contemplative mind.

XXXII

Osho - The Quiet Revolutionary of Inner Freedom

In the realm of modern spirituality, Osho, born Rajneesh Chandra Mohan Jain in 1931, stands out as a profound and controversial figure whose introverted nature played a crucial role in shaping his revolutionary ideas on meditation, consciousness, and personal freedom. Though his public persona was marked by charisma and bold statements, his introspective approach to spirituality and personal growth reflects the quiet power of introversion. Osho's journey underscores how deep inner exploration and solitude can fuel transformative insights and global influence.

The Solitude of Inner Discovery

Osho's early life in India was characterized by a deep introspection and a profound quest for understanding the nature of existence. As a young man, Osho was known for his solitary nature and his intense focus on meditation and philosophical inquiry. This introverted inclination allowed him to engage deeply with the spiritual traditions of India while also questioning and exploring beyond conventional boundaries.

During his years of study and reflection, Osho immersed himself in various meditative practices and philosophical discourses. His introverted nature enabled him to grapple with complex spiritual concepts and to experience profound states of consciousness. This period of solitude and self-inquiry was instrumental in shaping his later teachings and in developing his unique perspective on meditation and enlightenment.

The Power of Quiet Revolution

Osho's teachings were revolutionary, challenging traditional norms and advocating for a radical transformation of human consciousness. His introverted nature allowed him to cultivate a deep understanding of the self and the mechanisms of inner liberation. Unlike many spiritual leaders who relied on external validation or public acclaim, Osho's approach was rooted in an inner journey of self-discovery and authenticity.

Osho's concept of "dynamic meditation" and his emphasis on the importance of experiencing life fully and without attachment were reflections of his own introspective experiences. His teachings encouraged individuals to break free from societal conditioning and to explore their inner depths through meditation and mindfulness. This quiet revolution in spiritual practice emphasized that true freedom and enlightenment come from within, rather than from external sources.

Challenges and Quiet Resilience

Osho's path was fraught with challenges, including controversy, legal issues, and intense scrutiny from the public and media. His introverted nature, combined with his unconventional ideas, often put him at odds with mainstream society. Despite these challenges, Osho's quiet resilience and unwavering commitment to his vision of spiritual freedom allowed him to continue his work and to inspire a global following.

Throughout his life, Osho faced numerous obstacles, including legal battles and conflicts with various institutions. His ability to maintain his focus and dedication to his teachings, despite the external pressures, reflects the strength of his introverted resolve. His writings and discourses continued to explore and challenge the nature of consciousness and personal freedom, offering new perspectives on spirituality and human potential.

Legacy of Quiet Transformation

Osho's legacy is a testament to the transformative power of introversion in the realm of spiritual exploration. His teachings on meditation, consciousness, and personal liberation continue to resonate with individuals seeking deeper understanding and inner freedom. Osho's emphasis on living authentically and experiencing life in its fullness highlights the profound impact that introspection and inner exploration can have on personal and collective transformation.

Osho's influence extends beyond his teachings; his creation of meditation centers and communities around the world reflects his commitment to providing spaces for inner exploration and self-discovery. His work has inspired countless individuals to embark on their own journeys of self-awareness and to challenge conventional notions of spirituality and personal growth.

Conclusion

Osho's life and teachings illustrate the profound impact that introverted qualities can have on spiritual and personal transformation. His ability to engage deeply with the nature of consciousness, to challenge societal norms, and to inspire others through his introspective insights demonstrates the quiet power of introversion. As we reflect on Osho's legacy, we are reminded that true spiritual revolution often emerges from the depths of solitary contemplation and inner exploration. His journey invites us to embrace the strengths of introversion, showing that profound insights and transformative change can arise from the quiet, reflective spaces within our own minds.

XXXIII

Amitabh Bachchan - The Quiet Titan of Indian Cinema

In the glitz and glamour of Indian cinema, Amitabh Bachchan shines as one of the most iconic and revered actors. His journey from a struggling newcomer to a legendary figure in Bollywood is a compelling story of resilience, introspection, and quiet strength. Despite his towering presence on screen and his substantial influence in the film industry, Bachchan's introverted nature has been a defining and inspiring aspect of his career. This chapter explores how his introspective qualities have shaped his achievements and contributed to his enduring legacy.

The Solitude of Creative Focus

Amitabh Bachchan, born on October 11, 1942, in Allahabad, India, entered the film industry at a time when Bollywood was evolving rapidly. From his early days, Bachchan exhibited a profound dedication to his craft. His introverted nature allowed him to immerse himself deeply in the roles he played, bringing a unique intensity and authenticity to his performances.

Bachchan's approach to acting was characterized by a solitary commitment to understanding and perfecting his craft. His ability to engage deeply with his characters, often spending hours analyzing scripts and rehearsing scenes in solitude, contributed to the depth and complexity of his performances. His quiet focus and reflective nature enabled him to bring a level of nuance and emotional resonance to his roles that captivated audiences and critics alike.

The Power of Quiet Determination

Throughout his career, Bachchan faced numerous challenges, including initial struggles, periods of decline, and the intense pressures of fame. His introverted qualities were instrumental in navigating these difficulties with grace and perseverance. Despite the external pressures and the demands of the public eye, Bachchan's inner strength and quiet resolve allowed him to stay true to his artistic vision and continue delivering compelling performances.

In the 1970s, Bachchan's career took a significant turn with the advent of the "angry young man" persona in films like *Zanjeer* and *Deewar*. His ability to portray complex, brooding characters with a subtle intensity was a reflection of his introspective approach to acting. Even during challenging periods, including a brief hiatus from the industry and later struggles with health issues, Bachchan's quiet determination and inner resilience helped him make a triumphant return to cinema.

Challenges and Quiet Resilience

Amitabh Bachchan's career is a testament to the power of resilience and perseverance. In the early 2000s, he faced a significant career downturn and personal health issues. His introverted nature played a key role in his ability to cope with these challenges quietly and effectively. Rather than seeking public sympathy or engaging in self-promotion, Bachchan focused on his recovery and reinvention.

His return to the limelight with a series of successful films and television shows demonstrated the strength of his introverted resolve. Bachchan's ability to reinvent himself while maintaining his dignity and focus highlights how introversion can be a source of quiet strength and personal growth.

Legacy of Quiet Influence

Amitabh Bachchan's legacy extends far beyond his filmography. His contributions to Indian cinema, his philanthropic efforts, and his role as a mentor to younger actors reflect the depth and breadth of his influence. Bachchan's quiet approach to his work—marked by humility, introspection, and a commitment to excellence—has inspired countless individuals both within and outside the film industry.

His involvement in social causes and his advocacy for various philanthropic initiatives underscore his dedication to using his platform for the greater good. Bachchan's efforts to support education, healthcare, and disaster relief demonstrate how introverted qualities such as thoughtfulness and empathy can drive meaningful social change.

Conclusion

Amitabh Bachchan's story is a powerful illustration of how introversion can be a source of profound strength and influence. His journey from a struggling actor to a cinematic legend reflects the quiet determination, introspective focus, and resilience that define his career. Bachchan's ability to navigate challenges with grace, to deliver deeply impactful performances, and to contribute to society through his philanthropic work highlights the transformative power of introverted qualities. His life and legacy remind us that true greatness often emerges from the quiet spaces of inner reflection and dedicated craftsmanship, offering inspiration to those who embrace the strengths of introversion in their own journeys.

XXXIV

Ratan Tata - The Quiet Architect of a Legacy

In the realm of Indian business, few figures are as revered as Ratan Tata, the former chairman of Tata Sons and the Tata Group. His journey from a young executive to the head of one of India's most esteemed conglomerates is a compelling testament to the power of introversion and spiritual integrity in leadership. Despite his prominent public role, Tata's introverted nature has been a cornerstone of his approach to business and philanthropy, embodying a quiet strength that has profoundly shaped his legacy.

The Solitude of Thoughtful Leadership

Ratan Tata, born on December 28, 1937, into the influential Tata family, exhibited a contemplative and reserved nature from an early age. Unlike many leaders who thrive on public recognition and assertive presence, Tata's introverted qualities have been characterized by deep introspection and a thoughtful approach to decision-making. His leadership style reflects a preference for listening, observing, and understanding before taking action.

As Tata assumed leadership of the Tata Group in 1991, he faced the daunting task of steering the conglomerate through a period of economic liberalization and global competition. Tata's introverted nature allowed him to navigate these challenges with a calm and steady hand, prioritizing long-term vision and sustainable growth over short-term gains. His approach was marked by a deep sense of responsibility and a commitment to the values that have long been associated with the Tata name.

The Power of Quiet Resilience

Tata's career was not without its challenges. The Tata Group faced numerous obstacles, including economic downturns, competitive pressures, and the need to innovate in a rapidly changing global market. Tata's ability to maintain a low profile while tackling these challenges is a testament to his introverted resilience. Rather than seeking the spotlight or engaging in public disputes, Tata focused on quietly building and strengthening the company's core values and strategic vision.

One of Tata's most notable achievements was the acquisition of Corus Steel and Jaguar Land Rover, a bold move that demonstrated his long-term vision and strategic foresight. These acquisitions were driven by a deep understanding of the global market and a commitment to expanding the Tata Group's reach while staying true to its ethical standards. Tata's ability to navigate complex negotiations and make strategic decisions with a quiet confidence highlights the strength of his introverted approach.

Challenges and Quiet Determination

Throughout his tenure, Tata faced various personal and professional challenges, including the need to address issues within the conglomerate and adapt to evolving market conditions. His introverted nature played a crucial role in how he addressed these challenges—by focusing on careful analysis, thoughtful consultation, and a commitment to ethical leadership.

Tata's quiet determination was particularly evident during times of crisis. For instance, his handling of the aftermath of the 2008 Mumbai terrorist attacks, which included Tata Group's support for affected employees and the broader community, reflected his deep sense of responsibility and empathy. His approach to leadership during these challenging times was characterized by a calm demeanor and a focus on providing support and solutions rather than seeking public acclaim.

Legacy of Introverted Wisdom

Ratan Tata's legacy is a powerful testament to the impact of introverted qualities in leadership. His emphasis on ethical business practices, social responsibility, and long-term vision has left an indelible mark on the Tata Group and the broader business world. Tata's commitment to philanthropy, including significant contributions to education, healthcare, and community development, reflects his belief in using business success for the greater good.

The Tata Trusts, which Tata has been deeply involved with, embody his dedication to social causes and community welfare. His introverted nature has allowed him to focus on creating meaningful impact through thoughtful and strategic initiatives, demonstrating that true leadership is often characterized by a quiet commitment to making a difference.

Conclusion

Ratan Tata's story is a profound illustration of how introversion can be a source of strength and inspiration in leadership. His journey from a reserved young executive to a globally respected business leader exemplifies the power of introspection, resilience, and ethical integrity. Tata's ability to lead with quiet determination and to prioritize values over visibility has shaped a legacy that continues to inspire future generations. His life and work remind us that the most enduring impact often emerges from the quiet strength of introspective leadership, where true greatness is defined not by the volume of one's voice but by the depth of one's commitment and the authenticity of one's actions.

***

In every breath, they rise, they grow,
A living testament to the flow.
For those who dare to be unique,
The universe bends to what they seek.

***

Not in the clamor, loud and bright,
But in the silence, pure and white,
Does strength emerge and courage rise,
A soul unshaken, free from ties.

***

With every breath, they heal the earth,
In their stillness, a sacred birth.
Spiritual souls, they rise, they soar,
A beacon of peace forevermore.

***

They are the light that leads the way,
A quiet force that won't decay.
In love, in truth, they find their call,
For they are 'one' with all.

***

So let the world be loud and wide,
The introvert, their spirit guides,
In stillness, they are bold, profound—
In silence, they are deeply found.

THE END

About The Author

Paromita Ganguli is an Indian Author of the much loved poetry book - *'Starseed Epiphanies'*. For which she was honored with the prestigious '21st Century Emily Dickinson Award' in 2024.

Her narratives revolve around questioning the norm as well as offering an interesting insight for the mainstream to think out of the box. There is always a subtle 'spiritual flare' in her writings due to her perception of the world being multi-faceted and not just what is visible to the eye.

Beyond her literary endeavors, Paromita also takes great interest in volunteering and charity. She has volunteered for renowned organizations such as - HelpAge India, CRY (Child Rights & You) etc.

'The Divine Significance of being an Introvert' is her first non-fiction work and tries to convey her unique ideology that is long time due to reach the world and make it think differently.

Share Your Thoughts With Me!

Instagram handle: @guided_by_the_cosmos
Email ID: mitaganguli7777@gmail.com